Praise for Lifeline 65

"Fundamental to school communities is building school-family partnerships that foster teacher-student relationships. Students who feel connected to their teachers are more engaged, more dedicated, and more motivated about their education because they feel safe, supported, and nurtured. Ryan Stein's book, *Lifeline 65*, is a primer for educators who are seeking to enthusiastically make those connections to ensure every student is successful."

—Dr. James F. Lane, Superintendent of Public Instruction,
Virginia Department of Education

"Humor, grace, and poignancy make *Lifeline 65* a powerful read from start to finish. This book will have a profound impact on any educator's mindset when forming relationships with colleagues, parents, and most importantly, students."

—Julie Smith, The Techie Teacher

"*Lifeline 65* provides countless ways to engage all stakeholders. What an inspirational way to teach and lead a school."

—Dr. Dave Myers, Superintendent of New Kent Public Schools

"Ryan Stein makes the underdog the 'top dog' in the classroom and in every field of human endeavor."

—Dr. Herbert Monroe, Assistant Superintendent, Caroline Public Schools

"Mr. Stein always believed in me and pushed me to be a better student; he made me the editor of our classroom newspaper. Ten years later, that small amount of belief led me to follow my dreams of becoming a fashion editor."

—Madison Calogerakis, Student

Lifeline

65

How Small Connections
& Big Enthusiasm
Can Change Education

Ryan T. Stein

with contributions by **Jennifer Costa Berdux**

Brandylane
Publishers, Inc.

ISBN: 978-1-947860-59-9

LCCN: 2019942056

Cover and interior design by Michael Hardison
Production management by Mary-Peyton Crook
Jennifer Berdux's author photo by Isabel Lewis
Cover photography and Ryan T. Stein's author photo by James Waltman Photography

Printed in the United States of America

Published by Brandylane Publishers, Inc.
5 S. 1st Street
Richmond, Virginia 23219
brandylanepublishers.com | belleislebooks.com

Brandylane
Publishers, Inc.
Publishing books since 1985

Dedicated to all the students
we've had the privilege of working with
over the years, who have given us
purpose and meaning in our lives.
Thank you.

Ryan and Jen

CONTENTS

Foreword

"Children are not a distraction from more important work, they are the most important work."

—*C.S. Lewis*

Ryan T. Stein never stops thinking, planning, dreaming, or doing. As the principal of Greenwood Elementary in Henrico County, Virginia, he imagines big, works big, and motivates big. But if you take the time to watch him, you'll see it's the little things that really set him apart as a leader. Morning arrival is a bustling and busy time at Greenwood, and when Ryan isn't standing in the cold and rain to help students out of cars, you may find him kneeling on the hallway floor to tie a kindergartener's shoe, in his suit, offering up words of encouragement as he does.

Ryan has no problem rolling up his sleeves to get the job done. He's been known to stay late into the night after school events to take down tables and chairs alongside the custodial team. He spends his weekends writing grants and pitching corporations to obtain new playground equipment, new technology platforms, and even special lights for the cafeteria—all so he can create memorable and magical experiences for his students. He isn't deterred by the weather either—Ryan's delivered pizzas to students' houses on the coldest of snow days, and ferried boxes of books to them in the sweltering heat of summer. One day, he even stood outside in the blistering heat, holding a stinky runaway dog that had made her way onto school grounds, waiting for her grateful owner to pick her up. This is a man who can laugh at himself. Ryan loves to jump in with the school's drumline and straight-up embarrass himself during the talent show. He does all of this joyfully—it is his life's purpose.

I had plenty of time to observe Ryan during my year as his right-hand woman and metaphorical partner in crime, while I worked at Greenwood in the capacity of principal's secretary. I knew from the moment I stepped into that role that working with someone as energetic and enthusiastic as Ryan would be an adventure. But I never could have predicted how much he would ultimately influence me and quite literally set me back on course to continue what I consider to be my own life's work. You see, I am a teacher. I took the job as secretary at Greenwood during a time when I felt that I had nothing left to give my students—I was taking what I assumed would be a permanent break from the classroom. In less than a few months of working with Ryan, I realized that I had more work to do as an educator, and that I had to make my way back to teaching. I credit Ryan with giving me the courage and desire to do so. I got to witness, firsthand, the "Lifeline 65" philosophy at work and through that, the transformation of an *entire school*. Attendance at Greenwood improved markedly, PTA involvement soared, and test scores have steadily climbed since Ryan brought his philosophy of human connection to his school.

When Ryan told me the stories of his life that ended up in this book, they sometimes made me laugh, sometimes made me cry, but always made my day. And once I knew the stories, it all began to make perfect sense as I watched him set about his work to make connections with Greenwood families and provide lifelines for individual students in the process. He has been both the student desperate for a lifeline and the teacher equally desperate to find a way to be that lifeline. Ryan walks the walk—what he says he does in this book, he really does. His passion lies in the fight to improve the educational experience for all students and to inspire school staff to do the same.

In *Lifeline 65*, Ryan shares with readers his personal journey toward becoming an educator, and the adventures that have taken place during his time as a teacher and administrator. He shares a myriad of ideas that can be implemented within individual classrooms, schools, and entire school divisions. Start small, but think big, and do what is right for you and your students. My teaching style is decidedly different from Ryan's, but I have already used some of the ideas in this book to help me connect with my students and their families. You never know when a small connection will indeed serve as a lifeline to a child.

Get ready for a fun, career-changing read, and be sure to share your *Lifeline 65* experiences via #Lifeline65.

—Jennifer Costa Berdux

Introduction

"Nothing truly great can be accomplished without enthusiasm."

OK, so Emerson wrote that long before I did. But he wasn't the only great thinker who changed the world with that philosophy. Think about it: would Thomas Jefferson have been the statesman, author, scientist, inventor, and president he was without enthusiasm? How many lives and laws were changed by the enthusiasm and fervor of Dr. Martin Luther King Jr.'s "I Have a Dream" speech? Nobody would have wanted to "be like Mike" if Michael Jordan hadn't persevered and attacked the basketball court with enthusiasm. How many people could Mother Teresa have saved without her faith and enthusiasm to serve? Enthusiasm is the key to changing the world. This philosophy has served me well for the past 14 years in the field of education, and working alongside many incredible students, teachers, parents, administrators, and community partners is a constant source of inspiration and renewed enthusiasm.

Every morning, I wake up with the mindset that focused and direct enthusiasm can make a difference in developing the world that I dream of for my own children: a world full of love, hope, compassion, and acceptance; a world that celebrates our diversity and judges people by their work ethic, grit, passion, and integrity; a world full of respect, resilience, accountability, collaboration, and pride; a world in which contagious enthusiasm leads the charge in eliminating the fear of taking risks and expands comfort zones, as we create a culture of always striving for greatness and innovation; a world where our failures never define us, but instead lead to extraordinary achievement.

My personal story, like everyone else's, includes both losses and victories. As children, we can't possibly understand how certain events and the actions of others will ultimately impact our lives. Children live at the mercy of the adults around them and are vulnerable to the fall-out of adults' mistakes and failures. No one is perfect, but it cannot be denied that with rising divorce rates, increased domestic violence, unaffordable and inadequate child care, and rampant drug use, our children are suffering. From what I've seen within my personal and professional experience, a child's school often becomes an indispensable haven that provides some of the only constants in a student's life.

I had a great childhood. There was plenty of laughter and just enough zaniness to keep me on my toes, and I knew without question that I was loved. When I was in the fourth grade, I was a typical early-'90s student: my hair was parted to the side, and I wore Umbros, high Adidas socks, Chucks, and a variety of Chicago Bulls t-shirts; I listened to my Walkman, used my Skip-It, chased my brother with my Super Soaker 50, and spent hours outside each day after school; I loved watching *Saved by the Bell* to see Kelly Kapowski; on Fridays we ordered pizza, and if it wasn't delivered in 30 minutes, it was free.

In school we used transparencies, Trapper Keepers, and chalkboards and played dodgeball or tag on the wooden playground equipment. I loved *Number Munchers*, Scholastic Book Club, *The Oregon Trail*, *The Magic School Bus*, and scented markers. On field day there were winners and losers, and everyone had a great time no matter the outcome. I was a happy kid who loved going to school—but that gradually changed as my home life grew more complicated.

Sometime during the summer of 1990, my mother and father's relationship changed dramatically. I can clearly remember my mom screaming at my dad for staying out late and drinking. There were a few evenings when my younger brother would hop into my bed as we listened to them fight downstairs. Going out to dinner as a family would give me a panic attack. Traveling in the minivan in awkward silence only made the tension increase.

Eventually, my dad moved into another room in the house as my parents tried to work things out. It didn't help, and as the animosity between my mom and dad continued to grow, I developed anxiety. I started to hate going to my basketball games because my parents sat on opposite ends of the gym and would compete for my attention afterward. I didn't want to invite my friends over to my house anymore.

Then in the winter of 1991, my parents sat my brother and me down by the fireplace in our family room and told us they were getting a divorce. Even though this was not a surprise, it was still very painful information to hear as a nine-year-old. I put a lot of the blame on myself and grew a deep anger. The thought of splitting holidays, alternating vacations, and setting a schedule just to see each parent was overwhelming.

My father moved into an apartment complex about four miles down the road, and my brother and I switched houses every Sunday. To this day, I can still close my eyes and hear the screaming that would take place between my dad and mom each week. Eventually, my family decided to move the "kid exchange" to a public space. We tried parking lots, schools, and even our Presbyterian church, but it made no impact at all. Doors were still slammed, and the yelling continued. Pastors and deacons from the church would try to play mediator, but all this did was cause me to lose my faith in church, and I stopped going altogether until I married my wife 21 years later.

As a result of my tumultuous home life, my school life changed dramatically: my grades fell; I lost several of my close friendships with my classmates; I collected more tardy slips and absences in a month than I had accumulated my first four years of school; I became quiet, reserved, and did not want to participate in anything outside of school. I was falling through the cracks, and my teacher, school counselor, and principal did not notice at all.

Throughout fourth grade, not once did my teacher or anyone in school ask me what was happening in my life. I was never asked what type of support I needed. I never ate lunch with my teacher or played with her outside during recess. I never received a positive phone call or handwritten note. When I was suspended for fighting or received after-school detention for not completing my work, not once did my teacher ask, "What's wrong with Ryan?" I was lost, and no one at school noticed.

My parents did what they could to ease the weighty reality of their divorce on my brother and me. Our summer was filled with the stress of learning a new two-home routine, but time with each parent was now more valuable. We played more board games, traveled on vacations, and watched movies, and my brother and I even received a few spontaneous gifts from time to time. Looking back, I appreciate my parents more for how attentive they were to us in the midst of their own personal heartache. Ten-year-old me was just excited to show off my new Scottie Pippen shoes, Chicago Bulls backpack, and *Space Jam* t-shirt wherever I could.

It was that t-shirt that I had carefully selected to wear to the school open house that fall, where I met the teacher who changed my life completely.

Despite the efforts my parents had made over the summer, they still struggled with being in the same room together, and a classroom was no different. There, in the middle of the open house, they had an all-out screaming match in front of my new classmates and all the fifth-grade teachers. While most of the teachers and students either tried to calm my parents or avoided my family completely, one teacher focused on me. Mr. Decrosta walked right over to me, kneeled on the ground, and said, "I see you." He sat me down and introduced himself. Even though other students and parents wanted to meet him, he took the time to speak directly to me and get to know me. Right away we hit it off, and I knew in the moment that I met Mr. Decrosta that I would never forget him.

Mr. Decrosta introduced our class to many new things that first week of school, but the lesson that really captured my attention was when he showed us how to use HyperStudio on the computer. This was a new multimedia tool that combined text, graphics, sound, and video in one product (which was mind-blowing at the time). Mr. Decrosta noticed the strong interest I had in computers and invited me to have lunch with him in order to dive deeper into learning the new program. I can clearly remember his sales pitch because I have used it myself many times as a teacher and administrator: "If you practice hard enough, you can become the class expert and teach the other students how to use it." I was sold!

Over those frequent lunches, I scarfed down my rectangular cheese pizza and explored HyperStudio's amazing functions with Mr. Decrosta at my side. As he showed me different features of the program, we listened to music, laughed about shows we enjoyed watching, and talked a lot about sports. Sometimes we read books together, played a competitive game of Connect Four, or updated his bulletin board in the hallway. Mr. Decrosta even told me personal stories about his own children. Our conversations were authentic, bold, and upbeat and led to developing a more meaningful relationship between us.

As a result of his invested enthusiasm, I felt safe enough to tell Mr. Decrosta about my home life and the difficulties I had been going through over the past year. I opened up about the yelling and screaming at our family's "kid exchanges" on Sundays and how anxious I was going home every Friday.

In turn, I became more invested in his classroom. I volunteered to answer questions. I took risks with assignments. I met a new group of friends that I am still close with today. I read books that I still consider some of my favorites. I became an honor roll student once again. I was *me* again.

But Mr. Decrosta didn't stop there. Since he had learned how difficult my weekends were, he invited me to arrive at school an hour early on Mondays, before any other students arrived, to work on HyperStudio. Normally, I left school on Friday afternoon at three-thirty and returned at eight-thirty Monday morning, which was a total of 65 hours away from school. Mr. Decrosta went above and beyond to reduce the number of hours I was away. He made sure I did not have to go a full 65 hours without hearing that I was loved or that I could accomplish anything I put my mind to.

When I look back on this time in my life through the eyes of an educator, it occurs to me that on the surface, no one would have known how much I was struggling, or that I was in danger of becoming lost. Mr. Decrosta managed to find me by creating a lifeline, inch by inch, between us. He spent time with me, got to know me, and gained my trust. At the time, I had no idea how this one hour would change my life, or that this small act of kindness would help formulate my mantra as an educator.

This was the beginning of a philosophy that I would later define as "Lifeline 65."

The following school year I was lucky enough to have Ms. Westhead, another teacher who knew the weekends could be a difficult time for many students at our school. This amazing P.E. teacher opened the gym an hour before school started and allowed us to play basketball games. I can't remember if the games or drills were very competitive, but I can clearly remember Ms. Westhead checking in with all of us who took advantage of this open gym time. I remember Ms. Westhead bringing in breakfast and even purchasing basketball shoes for students who were going through a difficult time. In between pick-up basketball games, she sat next to students and told jokes and shared personal stories, just like Mr. Decrosta.

Ms. Westhead was willing to dig in and dig deep in order to reach each and every one of us. At a time in our lives when we felt invisible to most, Ms. Westhead let us know that she could see us, and that she cared. She gave us early-morning pep talks to inspire us for the school day. She helped us establish goals and implement personalized plans for behavioral and academic success. Most importantly, she made us believe that no matter what was going on in our lives outside of school, each of us mattered and had the ability to make sound decisions, even as we bobbed and weaved through our school days. Through her willingness to creatively and selflessly extend this "lifeline" to her students, Ms. Westhead's enthusiasm not only instilled in me a love of basketball, but it also changed the course of my life. I will be forever grateful to Ms. Westhead and the fact that she recognized the importance of connecting with her students as the 65-hour window came to a close and a new school week began.

As a matter of fact, I became very close with the guys who attended these open gyms. We practiced together before school, after school, on the weekends, and over holiday breaks. Any time we could find a hoop and a ball, we would play together. We sat next to each other during lunch, collaborated on school projects, and helped each other with homework. We traveled together on vacations and to basketball tournaments throughout the spring and summer, all over the United States.

Because of our closeness, our basketball teams in middle school (27-1) and high school (80+ wins) were very successful. I was fortunate that our success caught the eye of a small liberal arts college in Ashland, Virginia: Randolph-Macon College. It was here that I met the most influential basketball coach of my life, Mike Rhoades.

Coach Rhoades was a gritty motivator with contagious enthusiasm and a knack for making everyone around him better. He preached family, integrity, work ethic, and gratitude daily. He taught me the importance of always setting high expectations for myself, on and off the court. He used the basketball court as his classroom to teach life lessons and discipline. Coach led by example as he instilled a dedication and desire not to make excuses for failures but instead to use those failures as opportunities to reflect and improve.

As a college coach, Coach Rhoades was mindful of the number of hours we were off the court and away from the program. He knew too much free time for college students could lead to poor decisions. So he became a master of scheduling. He made sure we had a game every Friday and Saturday. He made us practice midday on Sunday, which made it difficult to participate in "extracurricular" activities on Saturday evenings. Our day off was on Monday, but he would schedule an "optional" five-mile run at five o'clock on Tuesday morning.

What impressed me the most about Coach Rhoades was that I never saw him sitting in his office. He was always giving up his time to be with his players. Whether he was eating lunch or dinner with a player, providing an individual workout in the weight room, or improving someone's jump shot in the gym, he was completely invested in developing an authentic connection to the people on his team. Coach Rhoades was a machine.

Off the court, it was evident that Coach truly cared about my academic success. We had weekly meetings to discuss my grades, and if I needed extra help in an area, he would find someone to tutor me; he even offered a study session at his family's dining room table. Coach Rhoades scheduled several conferences with my teachers to review my writing assignments because he always wanted me to improve. Returning to Randolph-Macon College on a long bus ride after a win, Rhoades would take time to check in with me and my teammates about our personal lives and families. He would even pick up the phone or shoot my parents an email to let them know that a kid from New Jersey who wore turtlenecks and leather jackets was somehow surviving in the South.

Coach Rhoades was what I would call a "Lifeline 65 master," and still is today. He takes great pride in connecting with his players, which is one of the reasons why he has been such a successful basketball coach—as I'm writing this, he is currently the head coach at Virginia Commonwealth University and was awarded the A-10 Coach of the Year.

There's little doubt in my mind that Coach Rhoades has made the impact that he has in the lives of hundreds of students because of his commitment to making authentic connections. He employed the Lifeline 65 philosophy even before it had taken root in my mind, before it had become the driving force behind my purpose as an educator, coach, and father.

The impact that Mr. Decrosta, Ms. Westhead, and Coach Rhoades had on my life is the main reason why I decided to become a teacher and a basketball coach myself. I promised to use my experiences with each of them to impact as many lives as possible. Their legacy of making personal connections with an authentic enthusiasm will be something I teach my own children, Bryce and Bexley. Because of these leaders, I now fully understand that relationships give meaning to our lives and are the key to success.

There is no doubt that educators have a lot on their plates these days. The pressure that accompanies high-stakes testing and maintaining accreditation status is brutal. Lack of funding coupled with the hours upon hours required to develop rigorous and relevant lesson plans can leave a teacher feeling frayed and depleted. I have been there—grading papers all weekend, missing out on spending time with friends and family because of countless meetings and emails—I have lived through it myself.

Now as a principal, when I walk into our school with my coffee in hand, I often see coworkers FaceTiming their children because they had to leave the house before waking them up. In the afternoons, I watch as teachers bolt out of the school building at dismissal time, not to head home or to hang out with friends, but in order to make it to a second job on time. I have seen teachers cry because they have never been able to be a classroom reader or a field trip chaperone for their own children, or they've missed their own child's award ceremony because their school schedule didn't allow for it.

Living the life of a teacher outside of school isn't exactly easy either. While most people get to "clock out" at the end of each workday, teachers have to remain aware that they could run into a student out in the community, too. I hide my drink at a restaurant whenever I happen to see a student. I've had to leave a concert early because I saw one of my student's parents. I once dove into a shelving unit at Target because I didn't want the principal of my school to see me.

I fully understand that maintaining enthusiasm and a hopeful vision of the world as we struggle to meet the needs of the children in our charge can prove to be a Herculean task on some days, and close to impossible on others. So I decided to write a book, to provide examples of how to create meaningful relationships throughout the weekdays, weekends, summer, and holiday breaks. These simple strategies can reduce the number of hours students are away from school (when that's needed) and add significant meaning to the hours when they're in it. Using even just one strategy from this book can ensure that no child goes more than 65 hours without having someone tell them that they matter, they are enough, and they are loved.

Nothing is more powerful than love, and when children feel appreciated and valued, they can accomplish anything. I am a firm believer that authentic relationships are paramount to student success not just in the classroom, but in life. Schools look to improve climate, classroom behavior, and standardized test scores, but none of this can be done without building relationships first.

Authentic relationships serve as lifelines among staff, students, and their families. These lines of connection create the heartbeat of a school. As more lifelines are created and strengthened, the body of the school as a whole is strengthened. This philosophy brings the focus of education back to where it should be, within the hearts of students. When educators work to build authentic relationships with students and their families, the educational experience is transformed, and reaches far beyond test scores.

Mr. Decrosta, Ms. Westhead, and Coach Rhoades changed the direction of my life, and because of their generous spirits, they have also made a positive difference in the lives of my students, the athletes I have coached, and the teachers I have worked with over the past 14 years. My personal relationship with my wife and the values I have instilled in my own children serve as living testaments to the tenacious love I received from these selfless heroes. By making an impact in my life, three influential role models have touched the lives of the thousands of people I have encountered in my life. The power and impact of an educator on the lives of our students can, and will, change our future.

Monday

Rickie

"Thank God it's Monday!"

These are literally the first four words I say every Monday when my alarm clock goes off. I blast out of bed, put on my Ron Clark and Eric Thomas motivational podcasts, and bump some '90s R&B tunes, all before five o'clock. It drives my wife nuts, but it gets me in the right mindset to attack the week. She is an extraordinary woman to put up with me and my predawn pep rallies.

You may be thinking that there is *no* way anyone wakes up that excited on a Monday. Even my own father didn't believe it until he saw it himself, when his visit in June of 2016 was extended to watch game seven of the NBA finals with me (Golden State Warriors versus Cleveland Cavaliers). This meant his stay now included the best day of the week: Monday. He had no choice but to participate in our morning pep rally, complete with coffee, motivational speeches on YouTube, music, high fives, and more coffee. When he joined me at school that morning, it was fun to watch my dad try to contain his smile as the chants, cheers, and music took hold of him (it was either that or the coffee buzz). Either way, he danced and cheered along with the students and staff and let me know he'd love to do fourth grade all over again at our school. I'm pretty sure that was his way of letting me know that he's proud of what we've worked hard to build at Greenwood. I'll take that any day.

There are two very good reasons why I'm so crazy about Mondays: my wife, and a student named Rickie.

My wife, Kimberly, inspires me on a daily basis, more than she knows. Her family owns several funeral homes throughout Richmond and Fredericksburg, Virginia, and she is the backbone of the entire operation. She handles the finances, customer service, and marketing material. She organizes the daily tasks, scheduling, payroll, and staffing. But the most important aspect of Kimberly's job is that she is the first person a family will either call on the phone or meet in person when they have lost someone they love. This is why I say my wife is the strongest person in our family, without question. When I come home and complain, "You wouldn't believe this email I got today!" or "Can you believe this student still has not completed one homework assignment?" she very calmly replies, "Do you want to hear about the six families I met with today?" Kimberly and her work truly keep everything in perspective for me.

In the evenings, Kimberly's cell phone will ding if the funeral home has received a call. You might think this drives me crazy, but it does the opposite. These dings motivate me to wake up and do more. These dings make me want to give more hugs and high fives. They make me pick up the phone and make more positive phone calls to students, teachers, and other administrators who inspire me. They remind me to tell the people I care about that I love them more often, because God only knows when my sand will run out. These dings remind me to make every minute count, and to live a life without fear and regret.

After hearing just one ding, the thought of calling a confrontational parent no longer seems like a tough task. After hearing one ding, turning in a lesson plan, an Individualized Educational Plan, or a data dig becomes a joy. After hearing one ding, attending grade-level and administrative meetings or an after-school activity on a Friday evening becomes something I look forward to instead of being just another thing on my plate. I have truly learned to appreciate my time to the fullest. Those dings give me a type of energy and enthusiasm that is difficult to put into words. When I go through a weekend hearing 10 to 15 dings on my wife's phone, I get up at five o'clock on a Monday ready to make a difference, ready to greet each child who comes into the building on Monday morning. My mentors—Mr. Decrosta, Ms. Westhead, and Coach Rhoades—did this for me, and set me on the road I would travel as I worked to build my educational philosophy of Lifeline 65. Today, those dings serve as a constant reminder to keep my heart, mind, and feet firmly in touch with that same road that began so many years ago, to make sure not one child goes 66 hours without hearing that I love them.

Over the past 14 years, I have been privileged enough to work with many incredible students at the elementary, high school, and college levels. Not only did these students manage to remind me daily that being an educator is one of the most gratifying careers on the planet, but they also reminded me that what we do inside the walls of our schools is a *calling*. Yes, these are the students we lose some sleep over, the ones for which we must move mountains and dig deep. But they're also the students who teach us the most, who force us to grow as educators and human beings. Some of the most rewarding and gratifying relationships I've enjoyed in my life are those that I've had with my students, and none was more meaningful than the one I shared with Rickie.

Rickie was an incredible child with autism who came into my classroom for science and social studies for three years as I "looped" as a third-, fourth-, and fifth-grade teacher. Rickie was passionate about these subjects and extremely intelligent. His favorite content was learning about the Civil War as part of the Virginia Studies curriculum. Rickie was an avid historian, and as a Northerner teaching the "War Between the States," I often leaned on him for information on generals, battles, and important dates.

Rickie and I had lunch together on Mondays and Fridays, which led to some intense battles of chess, checkers, or his favorite: history trivia. We even read books together and researched different people or historical events to go further into the curriculum. On Wednesdays after school I coached enrichment sports programs, and Rickie always volunteered to be my referee as he loved to blow his whistle to reinforce the rules of the game. On the weekends, we took some exciting field trips to battlefields and science museums, but his favorite trips were to see live reenactments. I can still hear Rickie intensely shouting Patrick Henry's famous line, "Give me liberty, or give me death!" before the actors could. For three years, Rickie and I were a team both in and out of school.

The best part of our relationship was, hands down, Monday mornings. As I stood in the hallway greeting my students with high fives, fist bumps, and secret handshakes, I would hear a flock of teachers chasing Rickie down the hall, as he ran from his bus to my classroom. I can still hear his laugh and the shouts of the fifth-grade hallway safeties telling him to slow down. I can see him bouncing into other students and even into the walls as his excitement for coming back to school on a Monday morning overshadowed the weight of his enormous backpack.

Once he made it to my classroom door, Rickie would stop abruptly and almost tip over. He would be out of breath, but he would still stand up straight and give me a salute. Sometimes he would just smile, but more often he would yell at me because he had a difficult time communicating; however, we understood each other perfectly, and no words were needed to express how much we enjoyed seeing each other on Mondays. I loved that young man with my entire heart.

When Rickie went to middle school, I cried like a baby. These were not tears of sadness, but tears of joy for all the academic and behavioral progress Rickie had made in elementary school. He was making new friends and seemed to be happy. I knew I would miss our Monday mornings, but I was hopeful he would find a special bond with another student or teacher at his new school. I was his biggest cheerleader from afar.

Two years later, on Wednesday, March 21, 2012, I was teaching a novel study lesson on *Johnny Tremain* when I received a text message from the school counselor at Rickie's middle school to call immediately. I stepped outside my classroom to make the call, and that's when I found out that my good friend Rickie had taken his own life.

My heart stopped. I stared ahead of me as I walked to the principal's office to ask for someone to cover my class. My eyes were flooded with tears and I struggled to catch my breath.

To this day, I do not know why this happened. I continuously ask myself, "What more could I have done? Should I have visited him more frequently or called him at home? Should I have invited him to my after-school programs even though he wasn't at my school anymore?

What else could I have done to connect with Rickie?" There are thousands of questions and still no answers.

In my classroom, and now in my office, I have a picture of Rickie to remind me of our relationship and our special Monday connection. Rickie has become the compelling reason why I am so passionate about what I do. He is one of the reasons why I felt it necessary to share ideas of how to engage with students and parents, and to ensure that funeral homes all over the world do not get another ding because of a student like Rickie.

Rickie's Tigger-like enthusiasm was undeniable as he came bounding down the hallway on Mondays, and it was contagious. Other teachers in my building looked forward to witnessing Rickie's arrival to school, and I'm pretty sure they were jealous of some of our elaborate high fives. One dose of Rickie's enthusiasm set us up for the week, and the next thing we knew, we were on to the next Monday. Rickie unknowingly created a wonderful rhythm and momentum for all of us throughout the whole school year.

Of course, plenty of what's in this chapter may be carried out on any day of the week, but for Rickie and me, it was all about the Mondays. By working together and sharing ideas for genuine connection with our students, we can generate Rickie-level enthusiasm and transform learning for our students every day of the week.

Pump Up the Jam

Mondays are a day to crank it up! As a teacher, my first purchase for my classroom was the biggest and loudest stereo system I could find at Best Buy. I would blast music that drove the classrooms next to me nuts. The walls would *literally* shake. But my students, just like Rickie, would sprint to my classroom after they got off the bus. When they entered my classroom on a Monday, I never had morning work, but instead gave them an assignment to dance, high five a classmate, hug a friend, or practice their secret handshakes together.

I was always picky about how my classroom smelled and sounded as the students first walked in. Creating an inviting atmosphere for my students was something I took seriously. On cold rainy Mondays, I put cinnamon sticks everywhere, turned the lights out, played some smooth jazz on Pandora, and projected a yule log fireplace video from YouTube on the wall. If we were expecting snow, I'd make sure we had a virtual snowstorm happening inside the classroom, sometimes set to the music of Tchaikovsky or Bach.

Several weekends throughout the year, I transformed my classroom into a theme that went with our unit of study, to create an exciting learning environment first thing on Monday morning. If we were learning about the ocean, I would bring in blow-up pools, fill them with sand, and have the students sit in beach chairs under umbrellas for the day. I played the sounds of waves crashing through the stereo system, projected a video of a beach at sunrise, and sprayed the students with sunscreen. One time I transformed my room into a jungle theme, and the video and sounds of the rainforest brought the room to life. I handed my students safari hats as they walked into my classroom, and since I forgot my bug spray on the kitchen counter at home, I quickly made my own bug spray with water and vinegar. The kids smelled terrible, and I even sprayed a student in the eye by accident, but they absolutely loved it and excelled on their end-of-unit assessments. The sky's the limit when it comes to something like this. Let your classroom reflect weather events, celebrate seasons, and become a magical place for your students to learn.

Students know when you truly care about them and enjoy being their teacher. When they feel you are invested in them as people, they are transformed into eager learners. They will perform better on projects, assessments, and tests. Troubling behavioral issues are minimized and often eradicated. Transforming the room for a special Monday morning is a simple way to ensure high energy and enthusiasm throughout the week, an enthusiasm that will catch like a spark and light the future fire of greatness.

When I became the principal at Greenwood Elementary School in 2016, my first purchase was once again a stereo in order to "pump up the jam." How could teachers *not* get excited to come to school with Lionel Richie or Taylor Swift blasting as they enter the office? How could teachers *not* get excited to come to school when they know they can wear a school spirit t-shirt and jeans every Monday? Our Parent Teacher Association (PTA) regularly provides a luncheon and coffee in the teachers' lounge to keep our hard-working teachers smiling. I have found that it's imperative to discover the "love language" of the people you work with and make sure it is clearly communicated and achieved. By doing this, you'll turn Monday into the best day of the week.

As a teacher and administrator, it is important for me to be visible every Monday morning. Therefore, I wake up at five o'clock to answer my emails, satisfy my social media urges, and check my schedule when I'm still at home. This early wake-up call allows me to be device-free for the first hour that I'm at school. I want to be in the hallways greeting teachers with high fives before the first bell. I want to connect and build authentic relationships with them as much as with my students. On a rainy morning, I've tried to bring sunshine into the building by wearing our school mascot costume and passing out virgin mimosas with gluten-free breakfast treats. On a hot day, I've shown my cool groove to the

"Electric Slide," and I've even split my pants when jumping forward to start the "Wobble." Thank goodness the students weren't in the building yet!

Pump up the jam at your school by inviting the marching band to play as the students get off the bus. Have the local high school or college cheerleading, dance, or step team perform for 15 to 20 minutes in front of the school entrance. Invite the chorus or string quartet to set a more relaxed mood during the state testing window. Ask the theater program to dress in costume and sing songs from their play to promote their weekend performance. Even something as simple as having a student musician or a member of a local church band play the saxophone, harmonica, piano, or guitar at the parent drop-off loop or outside the main office can set an upbeat tone for your Monday.

Our pride and joy at Greenwood Elementary on a Monday morning is our bucket drumline called G-Wood. These students wear their all-black uniforms with pride. Students open their school bus windows from about a mile away to better hear the G-Wood showcase their rhythm on 30 five-gallon buckets from Home Depot. By performing in the hallways and at our pep rallies, these rock stars inspire younger students to work hard in the classroom to meet the academic and behavioral criteria required to try out for the team.

If you're really trying to pump up the jam, you could even have your teachers and parent volunteers form a conga line of singing, dancing, chanting, and banging on the drums as each child enters the building. How could your students not be excited for learning when they see their teachers and parents holding motivational signs and acting like fools? Weekend troubles and even sleep deprivation for both students and teachers seem to disappear once you "hit the Quan" or "Nae Nae." The usual Monday slump, on what is typically the highest tardy and absence day, will cease to exist. Instead, students will arrive early to school. I promise that if you are looking to energize your school climate and culture, music is your answer!

Music is the heartbeat of life and the healing force of the universe, and when you pair it with a conga line of passionate educators, you can change the world.

Hollywood Hallways

I'm embarrassed to admit this, but I like looking at *People* and *Us* magazines during red carpet and Hollywood award seasons. I like to look at the faces and haute couture of the A-list celebrities and to think about the families and support networks that have played a major role in the success of these actors, directors, and musicians. How cool would it be to walk down the red carpet, just once, with people taking pictures, screaming your name, hoping for a brief connection or encounter? I encourage you to take that vision and create your own red carpet, or "Hollywood Hallway," at your school.

On Monday mornings, invite parent volunteers, retired teachers, police officers, firemen, grandparents, and all non-homeroom staff members to line up in the hallways and treat your students like movie stars. Hang a sign that says, "High Five Zone," and ask the volunteers to give 600 high fives in 15 minutes. Make Mondays the day your volunteer group assists with greeting students and takes time to sit and visit with them in the cafeteria. Create a high school mentoring program and have these young adults share their experiences, failures, and successes with your students. Ask your staff or teammates to create a secret handshake with each student and greet them at the door to set the tone for the week. Treat your students as if they are stars, and before long they will be, in every sense of the word.

At our school, we've named each hallway after our school's core values. Every hall is marked with a huge banner indicating its name for all to see. "Oh, you're looking for the lost and found? Take a left at Grateful Boulevard, make another left on Accountable Avenue, walk all the way down the hall, and it's in front of the preschool classrooms." Our teachers use 12-inch by 12-inch plastic sleeves with scrapbook paper inside to provide a beautiful background for displaying their students' work outside the classroom. The students are so proud to see their work in the halls, and this creates confidence and fosters pride in working hard to achieve excellent results.

You can really let your students' imaginations soar with different interactive wall ideas. To make a 3-D Lego wall, just bolt some Lego base pieces onto select sections of your hallways, keep the Lego bins nearby, and watch these dynamic murals change daily. Or find some wall spaces to paint bright green, and you'll have ready-to-use green screens for your students' video adventures. The possibilities are endless.

The teacher of the month at our school is honored by having his or her picture posted, and teachers and students may leave notes around the photo about the impact this remarkable adult has had on their lives. Our Wall of Excellence highlights significant awards our teachers have earned over the past 14 years. In the main hallway, portraits of each staff member are posted in black and white with a motivational quote to inspire our students. In the cafeteria, flags hang from the rafters representing the many colleges our staff members attended, so students can be inspired to dream big but also see college as an attainable goal for themselves.

Celebrating the diversity within our schools is paramount. Post flags of all the countries that your student population represents in the hallway outside the office. Post pictures of your current students and their families throughout the school. Create an alumni section and post pictures of students who are now having success in college, the military, the workplace, or at home.

At our school, we asked Michael's and other craft stores to donate quality picture frames. We used the app PhotoSquared to capture some of the greatest memories of each school year. Students are also encouraged to share photos of themselves holding our school flag while on vacations, weekend adventures, and field trips. This has really helped to maintain school spirit and to uphold meaningful connections among the students by displaying their shared experiences both inside and outside of school.

This coming year, we plan to hang an 8-inch by 11-inch head-shot of each kindergarten student in our kindergarten hallway. Then, we'll move each picture to the next grade-level hallway as the students advance from year to year. By the time this year's kindergarten students are in the fifth grade, every student in the entire school will have his or her photo proudly displayed, helping us to create a family atmosphere. Our hope and vision for this endeavor is that it will convey this message of truth: "We see you, we love you, and you belong here."

While envisioning and organizing your own "Hollywood Hallways," you may want to designate special common areas and spaces to recognize and celebrate success. At our school, fifth graders are the "seniors" of the student body. In honor of the class of 2017, our talented art teacher painted a legacy tree mural, for which our fifth-grade students' handprints were the leaves. I have visited several schools where their "seniors" have painted ceiling tiles or a bench outside on the playground. One school even had bricks engraved with the students' first and last names. If resources and space allow, use trophy cases and banners to showcase things like schoolwide reading success, PTA accomplishments, staff awards and recognitions, and academic and fitness milestones.

Honoring the creativity, hard work, and achievements of students and staff will help them gain the traction and momentum they need as they work together to impact the future in wonderful and meaningful ways. Creating a culture of success at your school will inspire your star students within it to shine brightly, each and every day.

Cookin' 'n' Crockin'

Having worked closely with eight schools in the past 14 years as a teacher, an instructional technology resource teacher, and an administrator, I have seen some wonderfully engaging events take place on Monday mornings. Pastries with Parents, Muffins with Moms, and Donuts with Dads are always community favorites. Breakfast Bingo with special prizes would pack your cafeteria. Celebrating Grandparents' Day with either a special breakfast or lunch is usually a popular event as well.

To go along with these events, our school has implemented Monday morning clubs. Students apply for the opportunity to create a year-long project with our art teacher or join the ensemble of students performing recorders, xylophones, drums, and marimbas together. We implemented Rubik's Cube, Math 24, Book Bowl, and Destination Imagination teams that all compete against other schools. Our basketball, step, and cheerleading teams participate at school spirit rallies and join in for our student versus faculty basketball game during March Madness. The positive impact our Monday morning clubs have on our attendance, discipline, and academic success is truly astounding.

Recently I started a new morning club called Cookin' 'n' Crockin'. Parents entered a drawing to win one of 10 free Crock-Pots and cooking lessons at seventy-thirty select Monday mornings in the cafeteria at our school. Parents submitted applications the evening of our student-led conferences and our administrative team conducted a live drawing over the morning announcements to pick the 10 winners. On the selected Monday mornings, these families bring their new Crock-Pot and learn to prep a roast, soup, pasta, or chili. Parents then take the Crock-Pot home and let it simmer all day for a nutritious and tasty dinner that evening.

The goal of this project is not only to connect with these 10 families but to share and create great slow-cooker recipes that busy parents can easily use at home. The ingredients for our meals are grown in either our indoor or outdoor garden or donated by local grocery stores. We've even had a few parents and teachers volunteer to lead cooking sessions. At the end of the school year, families who participated in the cooking classes will receive a slow-cooker cookbook to use throughout the summer, filled with secret recipes from our teachers and community. We will then encourage those families to post pictures of their home-cooked meals and come back to lead a class the following school year.

Cookin' 'n' Crockin' is a club that continues to connect and build intentional relationships with our community. It proves that our school cares about the people in our building way more than any test score. It is essential to invest twice as much time, money, and energy into making every child feel that they are significant than in teaching them how to answer a multiple-choice question.

I recently was asked by another administrator, "What has been the secret recipe to our academic success?"

"It's simple," I responded. "All you need are three ingredients: relationships, relationships, relationships."

Mentor Munchies

I t's no secret that children are significantly influenced by their peers in all aspects of their lives: social, emotional, and academic. In what ways can schools capitalize on this fact, and, at the same time, facilitate and foster the positive peer interactions that students so desperately desire? Educators can easily build bridges between students in their care by implementing student mentor programs, such as "Mentor Munchies."

In this program, younger students are paired with a student mentor to discuss different topics while eating "munchies" donated by establishments like Panera Bread, Krispy Kreme, or the PTA. Students tend to open up when food is involved. At our school, selected fifth graders mentor kindergarten and first grade students on Monday mornings in our cafeteria and classrooms. Parents of both the mentor and mentee have to agree to the terms of the entire program in order to participate, which include the following:

- Mentors must complete a series of training exercises with the school counselor to define their role and responsibilities.

- Mentors and Mentees must participate in five meetings after school.

- Mentors and Mentees must visit each other twice a week at school before the morning bell.

- Mentors and Mentees must volunteer together on a school project for five hours.

The relationships formed between these students have made a significant impact on student motivation. As both mentors and mentees continue to make attendance improvements and academic gains, our Mentor Munchies program will soon expand to all grade levels. I believe it is essential for every child to have at least one adult and one fellow student available to them at school, to serve as a sounding board, a soft place to land, and a lifeline, always at the ready, to help clear the path and light the way when things get tough.

Be Real

As a classroom teacher, it is imperative to find a way to connect with your students. How you do that is up to you. Whether you conduct a morning meeting, share weekend highlights with your class, play chess with a student during lunch, or participate in team-building games during recess, you must find a way to make an authentic connection. Whatever you do, remain true to who you are and do what comes naturally to you, and your students will love you for it.

I believe that the unique skill of developing healthy and meaningful relationships with students is the best attribute of a great educator and the very thing that facilitates miracles in the classroom day after day. Ten years down the road, your students will struggle to remember some of the lessons you spent hours developing and the thoughtful comments you left on a graded assignment, but they will remember how you made them feel forever.

Make Monday mornings something your current students will talk about 15 years down the road. Open the gym and host a morning basketball club like Ms. Westhead's, or teach a new computer program like Mr. Decrosta did. The bottom line is that if you strategically plan your Monday morning schedule, like Coach Rhoades did so masterfully, you can accomplish greatness. Put away the morning work packets and bring in a parent or a member from the community to teach your students how to monogram, knit, make soap, crochet, or design a t-shirt. Host a cupcake competition or a chili cook-off. Start the morning with a karaoke party, minute-to-win-it games, a Rubik's Cube competition, or an invention convention. Teach the students how to sew, design a bow tie, or use whatever other talents you might have in your bag of tricks.

Make Monday mornings a special event for parents, too. Have teachers and administrators hold up sidewalk billboards with positive messages to parents. Pass out a positive note, cold beverage, or a tasty snack to a parent in the car drop-off line. Invite parents to run around the track in the morning with a group of students and cheer them on. Have a coffee and hot cocoa station set up for all your parents who walk or ride their bike to school with their child. Something as simple as a firm handshake and an authentic smile of appreciation can go a long way. Show parents love and it will be reciprocated tenfold.

Start with one idea that will work for your school or classroom to enhance your Mondays. One child playing the drums or piano as the students walk into the main hallway sets a wonderful tone for the day and the week. Schools spend so much time and money to figure out why some students do not come to school, especially on a Monday. But I encourage you to dive deeper into what a Monday morning truly looks like in the eyes of a child. How do they feel when they get off the bus? How do they feel when a staff member opens their door in the car drop-off line? Students are not late to our Trunk or Treat event or our spring formal dance. No one is late to our evening PTA performances. Why? Because they want to be there. They can't be late. Make Monday something a child looks forward to, wants to be a part of, and absolutely cannot miss.

Are you willing to show up and be real for your students in order to create meaningful and impactful relationships? Cross the threshold of your classroom door every Monday morning with the resolve to reach each and every child in your class, even in some small way, before that 66th hour rolls around.

Do some of your students need a little extra from you, like my Rickie? The more you give, the more you will get back, I promise. The pain over losing Rickie will never leave me or anyone who loved him, although not one of us would trade even one minute we got to spend with him. You never know what life will throw at you or your students, so why not invest in yourself, your classroom family, and your profession to the best of your ability? Smile, laugh, and love right alongside your students, and treat Monday like the best day. You won't regret it.

"Authenticity is a collection of choices that we have to make every day. It's about the choice to show up and be real. The choice to be honest. The choice to let our true selves be seen."

—*Brené Brown*

Friday

Matthew

"Can't be shy on a Friday!"

These were my three classroom rules when I was a teacher:

Rule #1 *Listen to everything Mr. Stein says the first time*;
Rule #2 *Appreciate each other every day*;
Rule #3 *Cant be shy on a Friday*.

Now I know what you're thinking: "There's no way you only had three classroom rules." And you are . . . correct! In fact, during my first year of teaching, I had about 20 rules and we called them Mr. Stein's Bill of Rights. Over the summer after year one, I read *The Essential 55* by Ron Clark, and then I figured my classroom had to have 55 rules, but that didn't work for me either. By year three, I went back to the drawing board and simplified the rules to just three.

To fully understand the third rule, "Can't be shy on a Friday," I must take you back to my middle school days in Lawrenceville, New Jersey. I was an eighth grader, and I was preparing for one of the biggest moments of my life: the middle school dance. The song "Tootsie Roll" was just released, and I was planning on impressing a lovely lady from the Garden State with my incredible slide-and-dip dance moves. Every day for a week before the big dance, two of my friends rode the bus to my house to practice and perfect our routine. At that time, we didn't have YouTube to watch how to do this dance, but we didn't need it. We were ready.

Friday night arrived, and I put on my best pair of white tube socks, khaki shorts, and a white cotton polo. My friends arrived at my house at a quarter to five and my mom immediately drove us to the big dance because I wanted to get there as soon as the doors opened. It was not cool to be dropped off by a parent, especially in a minivan, so my mom stopped about 500 feet from the parking lot and let us out. We strutted to the doors with that New Jersey swag and busted into the cafeteria like we owned the place. Turns out the dance didn't start until seven o'clock, and since cell phones didn't exist at this point in time, my two friends and I were stuck setting up chairs, folding up the cafeteria tables, and carrying all of the DJ's equipment. I had a solid sweat going before the dance even started, but I wasn't going to let that throw me off my big evening!

By a quarter to eight, the cafeteria was packed. The boys plastered themselves up against the wall of one side of the cafeteria, and the girls did the same on the opposite side. The DJ took it on as a personal challenge to find a song to bring both sides of the gym together, but the sweet sounds of All-4-One, Warren G, Crystal Waters, Boyz II Men, The Cranberries, and even Coolio couldn't bring that parted sea back together. Then, he played "Tootsee Roll." The cafeteria erupted with the sounds of preadolescent screams and squeals as boys and girls moved closer together. The angel I was hoping to impress seemed to float from the rafters to the middle of the dancefloor and started to show off her moves. This was the moment I had been waiting for.

But I couldn't move. My back was stuck to the wall like I'd been Velcroed there. As the song played on, all of my hours and hours of practice went down the tube, and my mission to impress my dream girl was a total bust.

When the evening came to an end, I slumped my way to my mom's waiting minivan with my head down and looking as if my dog had just died. When I reached the van, my younger brother, Matthew, jumped out and asked me what happened. I told him the whole sad story. He looked at me, shook his head, and simply said, "Can't be shy on a Friday!"

At the time, I couldn't have known how wise he was.

Throughout my life, I have carried my brother's philosophy with me. It was a Friday evening when I managed to muster up enough courage to ask a beautiful Southern brunette to dinner. It was during another Friday night dinner that I asked this Southern belle's father for permission to marry her. It was on a Friday morning that I nervously and lovingly cut the umbilical cord that connected my superhero wife to my newborn son. It was on a Friday that I closed on our first family home, graduated with my master's degree, found out that my second child would be a little girl, and danced on the *Rachael Ray Show* on national television. Friday was also the day I had the biggest job interview of my life, as I pursued my dream to have a larger impact on students by becoming a school principal. That bout of painful shyness I experienced at the middle school dance ended up providing me with my personal mantra, "Can't be shy on a Friday." When I learned to get out of my own way, so many of my life's most meaningful milestones and blessings flooded in on Fridays, and because of this, Friday became my second favorite day of the week.

Once I began teaching in 2005, I treated Friday as the second-best day of the week in the classroom, too. I knew that my students were going to be gone for 65 hours once that final bell rang, and I wanted to leave a great last impression. I wanted my students smiling, laughing, and looking forward to coming back to school on Monday. This is why I high fived, hugged, or shared a secret handshake with every child before they left school that day. This is why we didn't take "tests" on Fridays, but instead called these assessments "celebrations" and viewed them as opportunities to show off our knowledge. I often wore roller skates in my classroom to symbolize the fact that we had rolled through another week! Friday was the day I would sometimes ride the school bus home, in order to build a more meaningful relationship with my classroom family. Friday was the day our students had to sit with a different friend at lunch and play with new friends at recess. However, the greatest part of Fridays was, hands down, the last 10 minutes of school, which we called Friday Celebration.

Friday Celebration consisted of a series of high-energy activities. Some Fridays we completed team building challenges; others, we had an ice cream social. Every other Friday, we had a flea market that was tied into our classroom management system. But the favorite of all the Friday Celebration activities, and an absolute highlight of the week, was when our classroom was turned into "Club Steino" for an all-out dance party.

Each year, there were several students who were just like the shy eighth grader I was back in the day. But in my classroom, I made sure every single student boogied. As a matter of fact, my students had no choice since "Can't be shy on a Friday" was a classroom rule. We learned the Electric Slide, the Dip, the Chicken Dance, the Whip and Nae Nae, Juju on That Beat, the Cupid Shuffle, the Wobble, the floss, and of course, the Tootsee Roll. We would perfect a dance routine of popular songs and perform it each year in the talent show. As Club Steino became more popular, we would even Skype other schools throughout the Richmond area during the last 10 minutes of the day so they could join the party. Energy and enthusiasm went through the roof.

I believe my classroom had perfect attendance on Fridays for a six-year span because of that third rule. It was time well spent, because these Friday Celebrations created a classroom family that was on task and engaged all day. We had no discipline issues and no attendance issues, and that is something to celebrate! Our dance parties strengthened our classroom family and gave my students something to look forward to each week. And to be honest, I think I looked forward to Fridays more than anyone.

There was only one time that Rule Three would come back to haunt me. It was a Friday morning, and I was teaching a lesson on area and perimeter. Suddenly, a little kindergarten student ran into my classroom and screamed, "Mr. Stein, we need you outside immediately!" This had never happened before, so I sprinted outside because I thought someone was hurt, or there was a stranger walking on the playground. As I busted through the doors, all of the kindergarten and second-grade students were standing in an enormous square on the blacktop shouting, "Mr. Stein! Mr. Stein! Mr. Stein!"

I thought it was incredible to hear over 200 kids shouting my name, so I started dancing in the middle of the crowd. But then I saw the reason why the kindergarten student had run into my classroom: there, in the middle of the blacktop, was an enormous snake.

I can guarantee you that nobody hates snakes more than I do. They terrify me. When I saw this 10-foot reptile, my hands started to shake, I started to sweat profusely, and I might have had an accident. To stop the students from shouting my name, I held a zero up with my right hand, and all 200-plus children quieted down immediately. I told the students and teachers that I had to get something from my classroom and that I would be right back. Nobody said anything as I hurried to the exterior door of the school.

When I walked back into my classroom where my students were patiently waiting, I was completely sweating through my shirt. I looked like I had been crying. My students knew something was up, and of course they asked what had happened outside. As I rocked back and forth in my chair, I thought about how I was going to get myself out of the situation. I told my students what was waiting for me on the blacktop. I told them there may never be another Friday Celebration, due to my impending death.

Without hesitation, one of my students stood up from his desk and started a slow clap. As other children joined in on the clapping, another student walked forward and handed me a yellow Wiffle ball bat. "Can't be shy on a Friday, Mr. Stein," he said.

Hearing my brother's quote was exactly what I needed. I grabbed the bat and headed back outside with renewed confidence. I threw open the door and waited for loud cheers from the students. This time, there was complete silence. But it didn't matter. I missed the chance to be a hero in eighth grade, and this time I was not going to let the moment pass me by. I squared up to this snake and gently tapped its tail with the plastic bat.

It worked. The snake started moving along the blacktop toward the woods. The teachers very carefully began to move students to the other side of the blacktop, without a sound. The snake moved about 15 feet, but then stopped. I looked over at the teachers and students and nodded my head with confidence. "Can't be shy on a Friday," I sighed. I tapped the snake again on its tail and it slithered again in the direction of the woods. As the snake got closer to the edge of the blacktop, the entire kindergarten and second grade blew up the playground with sounds of joy. Several kids ran to me with open arms and tears of happiness. But the loud sounds must have unnerved the snake, because he swung his head around and slithered back in my direction.

The sounds of joy quickly turned to screams, and I'm sure mine were the loudest of all. Students ran for the doors and climbed up the playground equipment. I even heard a few teachers screech, "He's going to die!" I was standing solo on the blacktop as the snake advanced in my direction. When the snake got about five feet away, it coiled up into an attack position. I don't know much about snakes, but at that very moment, I knew this was not an ordinary snake. This was a bona fide monster straight from the pages of *National Geographic*.

As I looked the snake in its eyes, I gripped the bat tighter in my right hand. I didn't know what I was going to do. But then I heard a loud chant from both the students and teachers.

"One!" I looked around confused.

"Two!" I remember the nauseous feeling in my stomach when I realized that the students and teachers wanted me to strike the snake. Reluctantly, I got in striking position and made my peace with the fact that only one of us was going to be alive after I heard the next number.

"Three!" I was ready for the final wind up, the *coup de grâce*, when the principal burst out of the door with a squad from animal control on his heels and screamed, "Stop!"

The animal control crew rushed to the blacktop with their snake-capturing gadget and put it into a huge plastic bin in about three seconds. As it turned out, the snake was the pet of a nearby neighbor, and was, in fact, extremely dangerous. Who knew? With the snake gone, the students rushed back to the blacktop chanting, "Mr. Stein!" I was Hero of the Day, without actually doing anything heroic. I changed my shirt (and underwear) and headed back to the classroom. Just in time for a Friday Celebration.

Senior Clap-Out

Mike Krzyzewski (Duke University), Bill Belichick (New England Patriots), Pat Summitt (University of Tennessee), Mr. Miyagi (*The Karate Kid*), Mickey Goldmill (*Rocky*), and Gordon Bombay (*The Mighty Ducks*) are arguably some of the greatest coaches of all time (real or imagined), but one name missing from this list is Virginia Commonwealth University coach Mike Rhoades.

Rhoades began his basketball coaching career at a small liberal arts school, Randolph-Macon College, and I was lucky enough to play for four years with him at the helm. I experienced firsthand the impact a coach can have on an individual. Rhoades has many gifts as a coach, but I think his greatest attribute is that he's capable of building a strong, connected family atmosphere that holds a special place, for graduating seniors in particular. Our most important team goal each year was to send our seniors out on a high note, which meant giving everything we had for the team. Our players truly cared more about our seniors than about individual accomplishments. Every pregame speech and every practice started and ended with the simple question, "Can you look yourself in the mirror and say that you gave your best effort mentally and physically for your senior teammates?"

Walking into the locker room years later as a coach myself, I carried this same philosophy with me. I wanted our team to focus on performing at its best because we respected and appreciated our senior teammates. If a teammate made a poor choice off the court, it affected our seniors. If a teammate received an after-school detention and missed a practice, it affected our seniors. I have found that when you turn the focus into performing for each other, your team has a better chance of accomplishing the unthinkable.

As an educator, I have continued to bring Rhoades' philosophy into my elementary school as I create a culture of celebrating and honoring our "seniors." At our school, our seniors are fifth graders, but at your school, your seniors might be eighth graders graduating from middle school or even 12th graders graduating from high school. I encourage you to think creatively about how to make your "seniors" feel valued, while instilling in them a confidence about what is to come next, whether it be middle school, college, or a place in the workforce.

At our elementary school, our fifth graders get to sit in chairs at all assemblies. They don't have assigned seats in the cafeteria or mandatory laps at recess. They get to take a senior field trip in a charter bus—which, to them, is the best part of the entire trip no matter where they go. Our "seniors" take a college tour and participate in a high school class of their choice for a half-day. We bring next year's middle school principal and even alumni back to our school to speak about leaving their legacy. We have a senior dance, a senior graduation party, and a senior spotlight segment on the morning announcements each Wednesday morning. Our PTA purchased a "Senior Class of 2018" t-shirt that our students wear every Friday.

During the summer, our rising fifth graders are invited to our senior camp. This is a great opportunity to discuss what it means to be a senior as they attend breakout sessions on being a "GATOR," an acronym for our school's five core values: Gratitude, Accountability, Trustworthiness, Optimism, and Respect. They learn about all the clubs and interest groups available only to them, our rising fifth graders. We do several team-building activities, eat pizza, and, of course, dance—because you can't be shy on a Friday.

Out of all these special activities, our seniors' favorite by far has been the Senior Clap-Out. This tends to be an emotional time and requires tons of Kleenex for students, teachers, and parents. On the last day of school (which, for the past 14 years, has been on a Friday) our seniors are ushered through the school for one last honorary hallway stroll, with a drumline leading the way, and Boyz II Men tunes blaring over the all-call system. All of the other students line the hallways cheering, clapping, and crying. Students make signs and banners as the seniors give their previous teachers high fives and hugs. As a final rite of passage, the fourth graders form a tunnel for the fifth graders to pass through, as they make their way toward our legacy tree. Finally, our seniors tap the legacy tree and head out the doorway for the last time.

What makes our Senior Clap-Out even more special is that we invite current high school graduates that attended our elementary school to walk the halls with our graduating seniors. They wear their full cap, gown, medals, stoles, and regalia from their high school graduation. The high school parents line up in the hallway and, not surprisingly, clap the loudest of anyone present. They take pictures as part of the "parent paparazzi," looking around incredulously as they try to figure out how it is that their babies are headed for college. Wasn't it just yesterday that they had started kindergarten in this very place? They express their gratitude for all of the teachers and staff who loved their babies along the way, with words, hugs, letters, flowers, and tears, as they look back and remember. Incredible memories are at once created and preserved with this one simple tradition.

Coffee Chats

Once a month on a Friday morning, our administrative team invites our school community into our library for a Coffee Chat to discuss a hot topic. These conversations have played a pivotal role in developing relationships with our parents and community. Some of the topics of our sessions have included behavioral strategies, how to help at home, internet safety, preparing for middle school, state testing preparation, social and emotional learning, gifted education, implementing STEM, anxiety, how to get involved, continuous school improvement, social media, and English as a second language. The Coffee Chat topics are developed in the beginning of the year by our students, teachers, and parents at our Community Priorities Workshop (discussed later in this book). The Coffee Chats are never longer than 30 minutes, but they can make a huge impact.

While coffee and donuts are great motivators, you may need to try different tactics to encourage participation in these early-morning Coffee Chats. Here are some that we've used at our school to help promote them and eventually make them a terrific success:

Get on the phone, call at least ten families personally, and invite them to attend.

Invite speakers, including local celebrities, community partners, representatives from the school board or central office, parents, alumni, or current students. Choose folks who can provide the most significant insights on the topic of your gathering.

Advertise your Coffee Chats by way of social media blasts, emails, phone calls, classroom newsletters, and flyers.

Set up live video streaming through various platforms for those parents and school partners who cannot attend. Email and post video links so families can tune in afterward.

Be sure to post pictures on the school website and other social media platforms and thank the parents for their contributions.

Align your Coffee Chats with other calendar events. For example, if your school is hosting a morning awards ceremony or assembly, hold the Coffee Chat right afterward. We did that this year by scheduling the chats right after our house breakfasts, and attendance skyrocketed.

Coffee Chats can be a game changer, and I have certainly found this to be true at my school. In some cases, they have served the purpose of breaking down barriers for parents who have trouble trusting the school environment because of their own past experiences. It is then possible for teachers and administrators to build relationships with parents who otherwise may have never been part of the school community. Everybody wins, most of all the students. What a powerful way to reinforce and strengthen the lifeline we can provide to our children, by getting their parents and loved ones into the doors of their school in order to communicate, collaborate, and thereby create a stellar, safe, and loving learning community.

Frolicking with the Fams

Hosting family-friendly events on select Friday evenings is a great way to stay connected with your students over the 65 hours they are out of your school building. I fully understand the importance of family time, and being a dad is my number-one job, always. By keeping families in mind, my school has held a number of really fun gatherings to which many on the school staff, myself included, chose to bring their own children. It means a great deal to me to be able to share these special times at school with my son and daughter. Being a dedicated educator definitely requires sacrifices, but with a little creativity and ingenuity, these sacrifices can become blessings.

The following list of Friday night events have all been test-driven at my school, and every one of them is always a rousing success. Each year, students complete an online survey to vote on which events should stay and which should go and to indicate how many students attended each event. We use this data to see how it correlates with our academic and behavioral progress. On the survey, students are even asked what bus they ride, and the school uses this information to determine what bus routes teachers and administrators need to ride on the day of future events to promote them. Remember, you can't be shy on a Friday. Get on board!

Parents' Night Out

Parents drop their children off at school for a student movie night, while they enjoy a few hours kid-free. Parents love date nights! It's an especially popular event if you host Parents' Night Out on the Friday before Thanksgiving or any Friday during the month of December, to provide families the opportunity to shop during the holiday season. Teachers and high school volunteers provide supervision, and once all the students are picked up, the teachers head to a local restaurant for some tasty apps provided by the administrative team as a thank you for giving up their evening.

Daddy-Daughter Dance

Dads, grandfathers, uncles, older brothers, stepdads, or any other positive male role model is invited to attend the Daddy-Daughter Dance. Ladies dress up in their finest attire and dads definitely dress to impress! Hire a DJ to blast some tunes or seek out the help of a volunteer DJ. Dads really get into the spirit of the evening. I've seen some dads arrive in limos and even party buses with a group of neighbors. The time together for dads and daughters is what this event is all about, but there are a few things you can do to make the whole thing wonderfully memorable. To make the night even more special, I recommend having a dad dance-off and lip-sync battle, or maybe a photo booth for dad-daughter memories. Our PTA volunteers had tons of fun creating props to use in the booth and running it over the course of the night. And, as always, provide some sodas and snacks. The possibilities are endless.

Moms vs. Sons Field Day

If the dads are going to have a special event with their daughters, you certainly need an event for moms and their sons! I have hosted an outdoor garden festival, community clean-up, movie night, and even a painting project with our moms, but each year our participation numbers decreased. This past school year, our school started a new program called Moms vs. Sons Field Day, and it was a huge hit. Moms, grandmothers, aunts, older sisters, stepmoms, or any other positive female role models took on their son in different field day events. The boys were split into their grade levels and we had some epic battles. The games we included were flag football, basketball, Newcomb, gaga ball, team handball, crab soccer, Quidditch, bowling, Hungry Hungry Hippos, and other team-building games. The winners get bragging rights for the rest of the weekend!

Talent Show

I believe that all kids have a special gift, and hosting a talent show each year provides an opportunity for your students to shine. Performing live is a great way for students to build confidence and to bring your community together. Students absolutely love seeing their classmates perform. In middle and high school, the talent show also provides an opportunity for students to showcase their staging, sound, and lighting skills. Promote your talent show early, encourage a variety of acts, and sign up a bunch of volunteers. You can even turn this into a fundraising opportunity as you sell tickets, t-shirts, and concessions. Finally, I recommend opening and closing the talent show with a teacher act and/or a father's dance act. Both lead to hilarity, without fail. Remember, you can't be shy on a Friday!

Student vs. Staff Basketball* Game

Who will dominate during this epic battle: the students or staff? This fun and exciting event is another great opportunity for your seniors to highlight their talent. I would select both boys and girls from a variety of sports teams, as well as other senior club leaders, to play against your (somewhat) volunteer staff members. Bring in the pep band, dance team, step team, and cheerleaders. Ask your teachers to perform the Wobble or the Whip and Nae Nae at halftime in exchange for getting to wear jeans to work for a month (or whatever works for your school and staff). Invite the entire community and, I promise, they will come. You may wish to use this as a school fundraiser activity or donate proceeds to a local charity. March Madness will have nothing on this game!

*If you don't have basketball players at your school, I would highly recommend hosting a Student vs. Staff home run derby, kickball, or beach volleyball event.

Trunk or Treat

Parents are always looking for a safe yet fun trick-or-treating environment for their children. Trunk or Treat is your answer! On the Friday before Halloween, teachers, daycare providers, and PTA board members park in a huge circle with their trunks open. Each grade level selects a theme and decorates their trunk (superheroes, Minions, Spiderman, 101 Dalmatians, Wizard of Oz, the Kardashians, etc.). The students and parents dress in their Halloween costumes and walk in a circle to collect candy from the teachers. There's even a DJ, ghoulish games, and frightening food provided by local food trucks. Safe, easy and freakishly fun!

Jazz on the Lawn

Jazz on the Lawn is an easy and relaxing event that can bring your community together. You can connect with local musicians to ask them to come to your school's playground and perform while your community brings picnic baskets and blankets. I have seen some schools that even allow a tailgate setup with tents, grills, and cornhole. This past year, I invited a middle and high school jazz band to perform, which made the event even more meaningful to our students and families. There are lots of great options for this cool and soothing event.

STEAM Night

STEAM is the acronym for Science, Technology, Engineering, Art and design, and Mathematics. Many schools are putting a sharper focus on implementing STEAM activities into daily lesson plans. Students love working on hands-on projects with real-life application. Our school took this new initiative even further by hosting a STEAM Night that involved eight different challenges for students and parents to complete. Some of the activities included Legos, slime, egg drops, robotics, playdough, and 21st-century technology resources. STEAM Night is a great way to keep your scientists engaged and prepared for their STEAM-filled future.

Literacy Night

Literacy Night is an absolute must! The purpose of this event is to give parents ideas and strategies that will help their children connect to the joy of reading. Teachers from each grade level host three informative sessions designed to provide parents with the tools they need to help their children become fantastic readers. The sessions will include the introduction of reading apps, writing activities, and sight word strategies. Parents are always asking, "How can I help my child become a better reader?" Host a Literacy Night and provide them with the answers.

Technology Night

My school selected the best student technology project from each classroom on all grade levels and invited those students' families to attend an awards ceremony on a Friday evening. Parents walked around our cafeteria and gym viewing all of our students' projects, while enjoying refreshments and light hors d'oeuvres. The students stood by their projects and explained how they made them. The evening concluded with our students walking across the stage to receive a certificate acknowledging their 21st-century technology talents.

International Night

Celebrating your school's diversity is important and enriching. It is a wonderful way to facilitate understanding and pave the way for a school community to become a school family. During International Night, families dress in the style of their heritage and share traditional foods with the community. Live, culturally diverse performances take place on the stage, while music that reflects multiple heritages is played throughout the hallways. Students sing songs that celebrate our diversity, and an Orff ensemble (students with recorders, xylophones, and marimbas) will help to encourage everyone to get up and dance. End your event by conducting a parade either in the hallways or outside around your track.

Family Fitness Night

Another favorite is Family Fitness Night! Students and parents rotate through five different fitness stations. These stations can be led by teachers or parent volunteers, but I encourage your school to reach out to your community. I have found great success in inviting the YMCA to lead a Pilates, yoga, kickboxing, or Zumba class. High school coaches and players love to come back to lead soccer, cheerleading, and basketball stations. Have the SEAL Team, fire department, police, or the Reserve Officers' Training Corps (ROTC) lead a station that will give your students a glimpse of what their specialized training is like. As childhood obesity continues to rise and negatively impact our students socially, emotionally, and physically, the importance of emphasizing healthy lifestyles within our schools is more important now than ever.

Science Fair or *Innovation Fair*

What if your school contains the next Albert Einstein, Isaac Newton, Madame Curie, or Alexander Graham Bell? Are they given the opportunity to showcase their love for science and invention? The Science Fair gives students the opportunity to research a scientific question that drives their curiosity. I recommend having students display their projects in the gym on Friday morning so the entire student body can view their classmates' projects. Host an awards ceremony in the evening to give parents the opportunity to view their children's exhibits.

Cultural Arts Festival

I am a firm believer in the importance of a fine arts education, including music, theater, dance, and all mediums of art. Why are students exposed to daily, hour-long science lessons but only one 40-minute art class each week? Not all of our students are going to be scientists, historians, or mathematicians in their jobs down the road. It is essential to provide our students with a fine arts education program so that they may discover their personal, and potentially professional, passions.

The Cultural Arts Festival brought all of our artists together. Students displayed their artwork while our musicians played light music in the background. Set up different stations for students to lead, which can include anything from face painting to bottle cap projects to sculpting. You could even give student writers and poets a platform to share their talents on a stage. End the evening with something light-hearted, like selecting a large group of parents to play an improvised tune on xylophones.

Moving Up Night

During the last few weeks of school, hosting a Moving Up Night can really set the tone for the importance of students remaining engaged with text over the summer. Moving Up Night is similar to Back to School Night, but this event happens *before* the summer break, and students and parents rotate to the grade level their child will be in for the next school year. This way, teachers can engage students and their parents by presenting highlights of the year to come. But most importantly, Moving Up Night provides the opportunity for teachers to show the parents where their students should be academically before entering the next grade level. Parents are then armed with the information they need to support their children educationally during the summer break.

Boxing Smoker

For five years, I coached at a private all-male military Catholic school in Richmond, Virginia, called Benedictine High School. During those five years, I met some amazing people and developed close friendships with teachers and alumni that I still enjoy to this day. This high school is a special place, and the alumni have a closeness that is difficult to describe. I believe that the special events Benedictine hosts on Fridays help create its culture of excellence and tradition. Hundreds of alumni show up to the school's October Festival, Captain's Choice Golf Tournament, and the Corn Hole Challenge, but the yearly highlight has always been the adults-only Boxing Smoker. This is an open bar fundraising event with five live boxing matches by local professionals. This event is an opportunity for parents to interact with other school parents and build friendships in a way that's different from just meeting at their kids' events. Tickets for this event consistently sell out in a few days.

Chili Cook-Off

Nothing brings a community together better than food. By implementing a chili cook-off, you are sure to get parents and students into your building on a Friday night. This would also be a great opportunity for your Cookin' 'n' Crockin' morning club to show off their skills.

You can even combine student showcases with such an event. It seems that when students are asked to display their work, they put more time and effort into a project. By overlapping a monthly Friday Art Walk with something like a chili cook-off, you'd not only have a time and place to serve all that chili, you'd provide your students with an outlet to share their efforts, talents, and projects with their family and community. Whether it's a readers' theater, an innovation fair, invention convention, a musical performance, or a debate, parents will come see their child's creativity and talents when showcased on a Friday.

By working in some Friday evening events here and there, we can minimize a child's time away from school and chip away at those 65 weekend hours—just like Mr. Decrosta did for me so many years ago, when he perhaps unknowingly provided me a saving lifeline. By extending the day, or bringing the students back on the occasional Friday, you could be providing that lifeline for a child and not even know it. If you trust in your ability to change children's lives for the better, you undoubtedly will.

Appreciation Song

As a teacher, when I felt appreciated by students, parents, and administrators, I'd put more time and energy into designing innovative lesson plans. I would beg custodians to let me into the building over the weekend so I could work hard to transform my classroom into a specifically themed wonderland, one that jived perfectly with the lesson plans I'd created for the week. I was more than willing to do this because my classroom family did a great job of letting me know that my hard work did not go unnoticed.

When I first started teaching, students wrote thank-you notes and gave hugs or high fives to show their appreciation. Expressing gratitude face to face was something that came naturally to them.

However, over the past five years, I have noticed that students at all levels—elementary, middle, and high school—struggle to communicate their feelings. Social media and the digital world have seemingly taken the "human" out of communication. These days, appreciation tends to be offered up by way of "Likes" and emojis.

It can be difficult to feel appreciated by a statement like the following:

Students need to be coached on how to have conversations and show gratitude with words and face-to-face actions. Giving a firm handshake and looking an adult in the eye is not a simple task these days for many children. I believe that table manners and dinner etiquette are just as important as learning about ancient Egypt. In dealing with this 21ˢᵗ-century dilemma, I have found it helpful to implement a school appreciation song.

At our school, the fifth-grade students are given the opportunity to write lyrics about their teachers and the reasons why they love coming to school each day. Our music teacher then writes a song using the students' input and teaches that song to the entire school. Five minutes before the bells rings on selected Fridays, our appreciation song is put on the PA system, which can be heard throughout the school. The students stand on their chairs and desks, and some even hold their teachers' hands while singing our appreciation song. Some teachers cry, but all of them smile. We also sing our appreciation song at the end of every pep rally and fifth grade graduation. This simple gesture has been an incredible way to show the teachers they are appreciated and loved, which in return creates a healthier and happier school climate and culture.

Appreciation song = 💯 🔥

Be Bold

Fridays are such an important day of the week for teachers. Not because of the occasional teacher happy hour that may follow dismissal, but because the 65-hour time clock begins the second your students leave the classroom for the weekend. Because of this, I have tried to make Fridays special and memorable days that provide encouragement for my students, so that they may return to school on Monday with a smile and an eager attitude.

Fridays are the day to break out the costumes: run down the hallway in a turkey costume the Friday before Thanksgiving break; dress up as a leprechaun on St. Patrick's Day and invite Irish bagpipers to play in the hallways; the Friday before winter break, impress your students by singing every song from *Frozen* in full Olaf costume; on Friday, May the fourth, be a stormtrooper or Princess Leia ("May the fourth be with you!"); dress up as Buzz Lightyear on your favorite movie day; and turn Dr. Seuss's birthday into a weeklong celebration, during which costumes may be changed up daily. On the 100th day of school, dress like you're 100 years old, and on the 101st day of school, be a dalmatian (or Cruella DeVille). I wore a 50-pound bison costume for six hours on a field trip to the James River in Virginia as part of a grant requirement on a Friday. I couldn't walk for two days after, and had a rash for about a month, but the kids loved the costume and I had a ton of fun.

Fridays are a great day to hold pep rallies or achievement ceremonies, throw your own "Club (insert your name here)" dance parties, or celebrate curbside as teachers and staff wave the buses off in a celebratory fashion. Fridays are a fantastic day to have group lunches, during which students have a voice in developing the class activities for the following week. Fridays are the best day to host a talent show. Over the years, I have danced with 30 dads to a pop song, rapped the *Fresh Prince of Bel-Air* theme song, synchronized swam with all the other male teachers, and danced as "Posh Spice" in a Backstreet Boys versus Spice Girls dance-off. You could start an all-male student group whose members wear ties on Fridays while they open doors for cars dropping off students in the morning. At my school, I call them our "Gents." Among other things, the Gents learn the art of self-respect and how to treat others in a kind and dignified manner. After all, isn't that what it's all about?

Host your book clubs on Fridays during lunch to promote your students' reading over the weekend. Book clubs gave me yet another excuse to dress in costume as a book character. I have been a pirate, mermaid, scarecrow, Chief Powhatan, Captain John Smith, and a dying soldier from the American Revolution. One year, my book club met on a Friday on our "lazy river" in the classroom: we sat on inner tubes facing the smooth waters projected on one wall, which made it look like we were all floating. Eating lunch was messy, but I didn't care. Instead, I blasted the sounds of the rapids and sprayed them with suntan lotion (not bug spray)! Several Fridays each year, I decided to keep my students after school to watch the movie adaptation of our book club novel. One time, our class took the cardboard boxes that the school's copier paper arrived in each week and used plastic plates to attach a steering wheel and tires to each box. The students then squeezed into their "cars" in our classroom-created drive-in movie theater to watch the movie *Johnny Tremain*. On Valentine's Day, our book club would get together for a "blind date" with a book wrapped in brown paper and tagged with clues. Flower petals filled the classroom and the sounds of Justin Bieber's "Baby" set the mood. A strong love of reading was in the air.

For no particular occasion, you could even turn your classroom into a "Starbooks." Brew some coffee (for the sole purpose of filling the room with that magical smell), don an apron, and have the children "place orders" for a tasty weekend read from your classroom library.

If spirit days are on Friday, wear those funky hats, tie-dye shirts, polka-dot pants, leather jackets, and mismatched outfits. Join the staff step team, drumline, or flash mob. Put on those tights and lead a Zumba class before the students leave for the week. If you're planning to establish incentives for your students to do their best on state standardized testing, don't implement the rewards and fun *after* the students complete the test—do it the Friday before they even begin. That way, while your students sit quietly at their desks for six-and-a-half hours, stressing out over a test that *supposedly* tells them whether they are a success or a failure, they can look up at your bright green mohawk or the temporary tattoos all over your face and crack a smile. Not just because you look ridiculous, but because you did something bold to prove to them that, pass or fail, you love them.

Host student presentation events to ensure that your students—and their parents—can't be shy on a Friday! Invite parents to sit on a *Shark Tank* panel (like the show) to hear their children pitch inventions they've created for different eras in history. Or have your students present mock trials to debate popular opinions or schools of thought within the context of their curriculum (for example: Should Captain John Smith get full credit for the survival of Jamestown?). With careful planning, and some help from parents, you can even host a cooking show. Students can make up recipes and record their cooking show beforehand, then serve their dishes to the audience during the Friday evening viewing. And don't forget about the classics! Poetry slams and book talks go a long way in keeping your students engaged and excited about what they are reading. Plus, inviting parents into your classrooms on Fridays will serve as the perfect lifeline for your families as they wade into the weekend.

It's hard to change lives if you're unwilling to place yourself on the frontline. Tell your students you care every chance you get, and more importantly, *show* them. Be bold when it comes to creating your Friday programs, because it will make a difference in your life as an educator and as a human being. And it will for sure inspire positive shifts in your students, as you build meaningful and solid relationships with them and their families. You can't make a difference until you make conscious decisions about how and when you will spend your time and energy. Choose to invest in love like Coach Rhoades, Ms. Westhead, and Mr. Decrosta did, by deftly crafting schedules that will reduce the number of hours students are away from school. Time waits for no one. The dings I hear coming from my wife's phone remind me of that every single day.

And remember that we became educators because working with children is flat-out *fun*. Enjoy it.

"Laugh at yourself, but don't ever aim your doubt at yourself. Be bold. When you embark for strange places, don't leave any of yourself safely on the shore. Have the nerve to go into unexplored territory."

—*Alan Alda*

Saturday

María

"I had the best time of my life!"

My three favorite words besides "extra bacon, please" are "back to school." To say that I used to geek all the way out over setting up my classroom each year would be an understatement. Hands down, one of my favorite tasks that came with being a teacher was preparing my room for my students. I took great pride in having an engaging and student-centered learning environment. It was so fun to set my room up in such a way that my students would become visibly excited about the prospect of spending nine months of their lives in it.

Each school year, I arrived about a month before the students returned to begin working in my classroom, like many other teachers in the building. On the walls I hung a variety of picture frames, which included motivational quotes and picture collages of my past students. Throughout the summer, I would visit every Goodwill store and yard sale within 25 miles of Richmond, Virginia, until I could add 300+ books to my classroom library. I even brought a sound system from home that would drive teachers connected to my classroom nuts, but I had to be ready for my Friday dance parties!

The last and final step to my classroom setup was putting together a 75-gallon fish tank, my pride and joy. During the first week of school, my students voted on the type of fish we would keep in the tank. Some years we kept a reproductive tank, starting with 15 guppies and often ending the year with over 100 fish. Other years, the students voted on a community-friendly tank, containing a variety of angelfish, silver dollars, and tetra fish. One year, our classroom even raised trout from eggs to "fry" and participated in a release party in the Blue Ridge

Mountains. But my all-time favorite fish tank collection was when my students chose to adopt a fish named Oscar.

Oscar was a 12-inch South American Tiger Oscar Cichlid, and he ate *everything*. This fish would absolutely destroy anything that was put into its tank the second it hit the water. He loved beetles, mealworms, shrimp, jumbo krill, mussels, and other small fish. All of my students loved watching him feast twice a week. They would rush to sit in front of the tank and chant, "Oscar, Oscar, Oscar!" at the top of their lungs before I dropped the live bait into the tank.

Except for María. María was an angel. She was a shy child from an amazing family. She was extremely intelligent, kind, soft-spoken, and thoughtful. She liked to dress every day as though she was coming from church on Sunday. One Friday, María ran into the classroom absolutely glowing, her eyes popping out of her head. She had a caramel apple covered in Reese's Pieces in one hand, and an enormous goldfish in a Ziploc bag full of water in the other. She had bought both items at the Virginia State Fair the evening before and wanted to give them to me. I knew what I was going to do with the apple because snacks are my jam, but I had no clue what to do with the huge goldfish. Therefore, after giving sweet María the biggest hug, I ran across the hall and begged one of my teacher friends to let me borrow her largest vase. As the teacher handed me the vase, she bet me 10 bucks that María's fish would not last until lunch.

She was right.

Around noon, I noticed that our new goldfish friend, which we had already named Bob, was floating on his back in the vase. The students in my class had not yet noticed, so I took María into the hallway to tell her about the situation. María was crushed, and her crying made me start to cry because I loved this young lady. I asked her if she wanted me to bury the fish outside or flush him down the toilet, and she quickly replied to bury him outside near our outdoor classroom. I told María that I wanted to keep this between us so the other students in the class didn't notice that our new friend Bob had passed away. María nodded. Then I heard a loud chant coming from my classroom.

When I burst back into the room, my students were crowded in front of the fish tank, and one was holding up the vase with Bob in it. Bob was flipped over and clearly dead as a doornail. The students screamed, "Feed it to Oscar! Feed it to Oscar! Feed it to Oscar!" over and over again so loudly that my classroom walls were shaking. A teacher from five doors down the hall raced into my room to ask my students to quiet down because her students were trying to take a test.

I turned to María and asked, "What do you want to do?"

Looking back at this moment, I should not have asked little sweet María what she wanted to do. I knew that this soft-spoken and shy child would give in to the peer pressure of her classmates. In fact, when María finally said, "You can feed him to Oscar," I already knew that's what she was going to say.

As I made my slow walk to the fish tank, I remember thinking that I had no idea what was about to happen. The goldfish was about half the size of Oscar, so I didn't actually think there was any possible way he would be able to eat Bob. As I took the vase from the student that I assumed started this chaos in the first place, I glanced at María one last time. She had moved to the back corner of the classroom. The students were now standing and chanting even louder as María nodded her head, giving me the go-ahead to put Bob in the tank.

As I poured the vase into the fish tank, the water filter's current pushed and spun Bob around in the water, which made it seem like he had snapped back to life and was swimming again. The kids gasped and then started shouting again. "Bob's alive!" they shrieked. "Bob's alive!"

María ran to the tank. "Save his life!" she screamed. I might have uttered an expletive under my breath as I grabbed for the fish net to get Bob out of the tank. Some kids were banging on the tank glass, others were crying, and most of them were covering their eyes. By the time I got the net into the water, Oscar was ripping Bob into pieces.

Despite the chaos that again erupted around the tank, I was able to steal a glance across the room to find María. She appeared to be frozen to the floor as she stared at the fish tank, its water now polluted with little pieces of poor Bob. Almost simultaneously, the noise in the classroom died down and we all stood there in silence, the useless fish net still in my hand dripping a puddle on the floor. We all watched María as she shifted her gaze from the scene of the crime to look at each of us. She seemed to be full of a question she didn't know how to ask. In her eyes, I saw confusion and something that I can only describe as a shattered sadness. Our classroom family surrounded her, offering up words of condolence and hugs. The guilt I felt at that moment consumed me.

As soon as I was able, I called María's father and told him what had happened. I was surprised that he was not as upset as I thought he would be, but I did not want to go 65 hours before I saw María again. I was ready and more than willing to make it up to her ASAP. So I invited María to sit on the bench as a "guest manager" for the varsity high school basketball team I coached at our upcoming game that Saturday evening. We were scheduled to play the number one high school team in the county, Oak Hill Academy, at the University of Richmond Robins Center. María's dad, who was a proud alumni of that team, was ecstatic about this opportunity for his daughter, as this game was poised to be one of the best high school basketball games in the past 15 years.

On Saturday evening, the gym was jam-packed with over 8,000 people! For an average high school basketball game, that was unheard of. Our team was undefeated and loaded with talent. We had four division-one basketball players and one who is still playing in the NBA (Ed Davis). Oak Hill Academy had even more talent, including over six division-one basketball players and two players who are also currently playing in the NBA. This was Goliath versus Goliath, Superman versus Batman, and my guest manager María was going to have the best seat in the house, on the bench right next to our players.

Throughout the game, I glanced down the bench to see María's huge blue eyes almost popping out of her head with excitement, as she watched the action up close. She joined in our huddles, passing water to players who were three feet taller than her. She came to the locker room at halftime and gave my team high fives as she wished them good luck in the second half. She cheered her heart out. Finally, with 4.4 seconds left on the game clock and our team leading 72-69, Ed Davis stepped up to the free throw line.

Now if Ed made just one free throw, our team would more than likely win the game. As Ed took his first shot, all the players, coaches, and sweet María held hands on the bench for good luck. He missed. The entire gym of 8,000-plus spectators were now in complete silence as Ed took his second shot and … *swoosh*. Nothing but net! 73-69! The entire gym erupted!

Oak Hill's best player, Brandon Jenkins, got the ball and made a 3-point shot from half-court at the buzzer, but it wasn't enough. We won 73-72. Our whole team rushed the court to celebrate beating the best team in the county. As I ran to join them, our big 6'8", 235-pound center grabbed me and threw me into the air with joy. But all things that go up must come down, and he had thrown me into the crowd of the other coaches and, yes, right onto little María. And boy, did I crush her. We landed in a heap on the gym floor.

On Sunday morning, the newspapers were filled with articles about our team pulling off one of the greatest high school basketball upsets in the Richmond area. I received phone calls from friends that I had not spoken to in years. Everyone in my family called to say congratulations on the big win. I spent hours on the phone that Sunday—but no call was more important than the one I received from an unknown number at around six-thirty that evening. It was little, sweet María.

I knew exactly who it was as soon as she shouted, "Hello, Mr. Stein!" I could literally feel María's excitement through the phone. "I had the best time of my life!" she squealed. That Monday morning, she talked a mile a minute as she shared with her classmates all about her courtside adventure. For a solid month, she wore the shirt I had given her that night and showed up to every basketball game after that to cheer from the stands.

During the weeks after the game, María began to come out of her shell more and more. The whole experience served as a kind of social breakthrough for María, because her classmates wanted to talk to her about her brief stint as team manager. She became more confident as a young lady, which impacted her academics and her ability to make friends.

I received so many emails from classroom parents asking if their student could join me courtside that I had to ready myself for a new tradition. I invited a guest manager to every game I coached for the next eleven years.

My experience with María taught me that Saturdays are phenomenal days for friendship and healing. Spending time with a student away from school and apart from academics can provide perspective, dissipate sadness and stress, and strengthen bonds. Saturday connections may not be for the faint of heart, but for those with a heart of a warrior, they can make all the difference.

Most Influential Educator

Do the coaches in your area preach academics first and sports second, or the other way around? In the phrase "student athlete," the word "student" comes first for a reason. But I have found that some coaches still put pressure on their athletes to attend practices over school functions like back-to-school night, a PTA performance, or even an afterschool study session. Some of the greatest youth and high school coaches I have known put an academic and attendance expectation on their athletes. These coaches have attended parent-teacher conferences and worked with the school to make sure they didn't host a practice or game on the evening of a major school event. They never made their team choose between school and sports, because the fact of the matter is that probably 99 percent of these school athletes will not go on to play professional sports for a living. These coaches are invested in the success of their players throughout their lives, not just on the court or the field.

As a high school varsity basketball coach, I made sure my athletes knew the order of my priorities for them:

Faith and family

School

Community service

Basketball

I posted these priorities in the locker room and in the coach's office. I set high academic, attendance, and social media expectations for my student athletes. We participated in three community service projects each year. If a player was struggling academically, it was an expectation that they miss practice in order to receive extra help.

In the beginning of each season, I asked the seniors on my team to write an essay about their most influential educator. The seniors selected a variety of educators, including a high school math and social studies teacher, a middle school principal, an elementary school teacher, coaches from youth recreation leagues, middle school coaches, and even parents and grandparents. I then contacted each and every one of these influential educators and invited them to sit on the bench as a guest coach for a home game. To start the game, each senior stood at center court with his most influential educator and read his essay to the crowd.

Think about your school and who the most influential people are in your building. In some cases, a football or basketball coach may have the most influence not only on the people in your building, but on the community as a whole. Encouraging these influential people to implement an academic- and gratitude-focused program would remind your teachers, students, and community that academics always comes first. It's powerful to see which teachers or past coaches get invited by your seniors to sit on the bench or stand on the field. And I can promise you, being a guest coach has a huge impact on the honored educators as well.

I know this feeling firsthand. The year I became a principal, I was no longer allowed to coach varsity basketball due to the demands of administration. To this day, I remember telling my basketball family that I had to step away from coaching, and then crying in my car for about 30 minutes in the parking lot. This was by far one of the toughest times in my life, because I loved my players as if they were part of my family. For a while, I couldn't sleep. I lost 10 pounds. I was fighting depression. Coaching high school basketball for 10 years had given me many of my closest friendships, and I did not want to leave it behind.

A few months down the road, I got a phone call from my good friend Matt McKeag, the basketball coach who replaced me at Glen Allen High School in Richmond, Virginia. He asked if I would sit on the bench as the most influential educator for one of the seniors on the team. He explained to me that this senior chose me not just because I had coached him the previous two seasons, but because I was his teacher in fifth grade and made math fun. I clearly remember standing on the court with the senior, listening to his essay, and feeling so proud of what this young man had accomplished. It truly meant the world to me that I was selected as his most influential educator. As a coach, I have won two Virginia state championships and many league titles, won rival games at the buzzer, and beat the number one team in the nation. But my favorite coaching memory will always be sitting on the bench as guest coach for a regular season game. Thank you, Jamal! I will never forget that incredible moment.

Be Well Program

Implementing a Be Well program, which seeks to motivate students to be active and make healthy choices, is simple, but powerful. The first step I took at Greenwood Elementary School was to give all students an opportunity to run around the track during recess. I'm also in the process of working out a schedule that will allow one grade level each morning to use the track before the late bell rings, in order to get our students to be active the minute they arrive at school. The students collect a straw for every lap they run, and their teacher records each child's total laps. In the classroom, our teachers post the number of laps each child runs and as a school, we give "toe tokens" as incentives for reaching milestones (25, 50, 75, 100, 125, 150, and 200 miles). Toe tokens are keychains with tiny plastic shoes in a variety of colors that represent the different milestones. Students can attach their tokens to their backpacks to show them off. We purchased a perpetual plaque to post the names of the top five runners for the year in our Hollywood Hallways.

Our Be Well program included the implementation of an innovative cycling room with a pedal-a-watt system, which converts the energy generated from pedaling into electricity. Our students not only get a great workout, but they are able to power cell phones, music, our indoor tower gardens, and a popcorn machine. It's no secret that children need to move and in fact learn more when they are afforded the opportunity to do so. In plenty of school systems, recess is either being shortened or done away with, and formal physical education classes only take place once or twice a week. In our cycling room, students are able to burn off excess energy, feel empowered as they see their work converted into usable wattage, and learn a thing or two about electricity while they're at it.

In another effort to minimize the 65 hours the students are off campus, our school has implemented a Saturday morning running club. This program, Gators on the Go, is open to current students, alumni, parents, teachers, and community partners. As the Be Well program continues to help students focus on fitness and health, we use the Saturday morning runs to increase their endurance in preparation for our Turkey Trot around Thanksgiving, and the mile-long Kid Fun Run, held in April on Monument Avenue in Richmond. I'm working to partner with local businesses to provide t-shirts, water, and snacks at practices and on race days. I brought this idea from the first school I worked at for five years, Echo Lake Elementary School. Their Saturday morning running club called themselves the Weekend Warriors. This running program started with about 25 runners but has now grown to almost 200.

When the program was first getting started, I wanted to help motivate more students to join. So on the Friday before the big Saturday morning race, another teacher and I decided to dress up as the tortoise and the hare for school. All 600 students were lined up outside on the bus loop when I busted out of the front door in a full-blown Easter Bunny costume. Just like the fable, I ran fast out of the gate and took a convincing lead on the tortoise. I gave students and teachers high fives and hugs, while the tortoise slowly and steadily trotted along, undistracted. I did push-ups and sit-ups in the middle of the bus loop and the kids cheered loudly as the tortoise eventually passed me.

I jumped up to start running again. But with that movement, the forehead strap inside my mask snapped loose and whipped down my face, slicing a three-inch cut across my nose. I did not notice it at the time, but blood started pouring down my face and onto the fluffy white chest of the bunny costume. While I ran to catch up with the tortoise, I heard students let out horrified screams, but assumed they were wild cheers. I tried to give out high fives along the way, but kids ran away crying. Teachers were shouting at me, "Ryan! Go inside now!" I had no idea what was wrong. I kept running.

Once I completed the race in second place, the principal quickly ushered me inside the building. Before the door could even close behind us, she took off my bunny head and that's when I saw the absolute panic on her face. I looked down at my costume. It looked like the bunny was shot in the chest. It must have been completely terrifying.

We got 75 more runners to join the Weekend Warriors the following year.

As the club continued to grow, I noticed that parents who had never met before were developing friendships. Play dates were being planned for the students. Friendships across grade levels were being formed. Student mentorships were happening right in front of my eyes. Throughout the week, Weekend Warriors members looked out for each other. They sat together during lunch and played together during recess. Students gave appreciative hugs and high fives to the teachers who gave up their Saturday mornings to run a mile around the track at school. The running club formed into a family.

In 2010, I received a heartbreaking phone call from my mother. She told me she was diagnosed with breast cancer and would have to get a mastectomy immediately. My mother and I are extremely close, and this news was devastating. I tried to hide my pain at work, but kids know when something is wrong.

About a month after the call, I traveled to New Jersey to be by her side during the surgery and assure her that everything would be OK. As I sat in the lobby for the longest three hours of my life, I prayed and prayed. When the doctor came back into the lobby and told me the surgery went great, the relief I felt is difficult to put into words. When I saw my mother, I must have held her for 20 minutes.

I decided to drive back to Virginia on a Friday night since my brother and my mom's close friends were going to help her start the process for recovery. I didn't get home until 1 in the morning and I struggled to sleep. As a matter of fact, I don't know if I slept more than 30 minutes that night. Instead of staying in my bed all day, I decided to join the running club at 9 o'clock that morning I put my shoes on and headed out the door towards Echo Lake Elementary School.

As I pulled up to the school, the parking lot was packed. I rushed toward the track because I was a few minutes late. As I ran closer, I noticed that the students had the same orange shirt on. When I arrived at the track, I looked more closely at the shirts. "In Honor of Karla Stein," they read. I started crying on the spot. My coworker and organizer of the running club, Heather Reid, had worked with a t-shirt company to print the shirts, and the show of solidarity made such an impact on my life. I called my mother after running and demanded that she recover quickly, in order to come to Virginia to cheer on the club in the mile-long Kid Fun Run in their new orange shirts. This put a big smile on my mother's face, and she was determined to make it happen. A few months down the road, my brother drove her down to Virginia, and Karla Stein cheered her heart out for the orange-clad Weekend Warriors.

Gator Gardens

The Gator Gardens at my school is developing into something special. I started an initiative to grow the foods that students and staff eat in school lunches, to promote healthy choices. We purchased tower gardens, which utilize aeroponic technology much like NASA's to grow food indoors, without soil. We planted lettuce, cabbage, spinach, and herbs. Within a few weeks, our towers were ready for the first harvest, and what the towers yielded was then served in our cafeteria in the form of salads for the whole student body. We have since brought in food trucks to show our students different recipes that use the greens grown in the towers. Students have completed measurement activities and expository writings in correlation with their growing and culinary efforts. Our art teacher incorporated the herbs into her students' pottery projects. Before holiday breaks, we often put our greens into large gallon trash bags and share them with families in the community, turning our school's indoor garden into a powerful community program.

Outside in the Gator Gardens, we maintain a beautiful butterfly garden that attracts the monarchs that our kindergarten and first grade teachers grow from larvae each year. We have several herb beds that grow beautifully during the spring and summer. Near the end of the summer and again at the beginning of spring, our students plant a variety of fruits and vegetables, which are then harvested for months and combined with the greens from our tower gardens to make loads of colorful and healthy creations, including smoothies for the teachers' lounge.

Our school also partnered with a nonprofit organization, called Jacob's Chance, which provides inclusive social and sports programs for children, teens, and young adults with disabilities here in Richmond, Virginia. Several garden beds within our Gator Gardens are designated for Jacob's Chance participants. We even designed raised beds that are wheelchair accessible. On Saturday mornings, these students have spent hours in our garden, planting, touching, and smelling the herbs and vegetables.

Our school has also added a technology component to our Gator Gardens with the purchase of several 3-D printers. With these printers we've designed and printed our own 3-D tools, weather instruments, and bird houses. We designed vegetable pencil toppers that are sold as a fundraiser for new plants and seeds. We even printed and posted QR codes throughout the garden that, when scanned, provide more information about the herbs, plants, and vegetables.

As the Gator Gardens and our nutrition program continue to grow, my hope is to eventually grow enough produce to set up a farmer's market for our community. We have applied for grants that would help us power our tower gardens through solar energy and pedal power, establishing a cycling room where students would pedal bikes to generate enough power to run the entire indoor garden system (saving us hundreds of dollars on our energy bill). Our end goal is to have all of our students involved in growing their own food, in the hopes that this will lead to a lifelong understanding of food and nutrition.

The Gator Gardens and the Be Well programs tie in beautifully with the Lifeline 65 mindset. These are initiatives that teach our students life skills they will have at their disposal forever, well beyond the classroom walls. What good is a philosophy like Lifeline 65 if it doesn't emphasize the importance of self-care and self-sufficiency? Sometimes you have to be your own lifeline, and programs like these teach our children just that.

Spirit Night

"We got spirit, yes we do! We got spirit, how 'bout you?"

I f you asked your students to perform a school cheer, would they be enthusiastic? What would the energy be like if you asked a group of teachers to lead a cheer at a faculty meeting, pep rally, or back-to-school night? Would they be enthusiastic, or would they complain about not having enough time in their classrooms? Would your spirit leaders shine their contagious enthusiasm, or would they be afraid to step into the light? It's important to put a lot of thought into your school climate and culture because it directly correlates to student and teacher success.

I have always surrounded myself with people who not only look forward to cheers and chants, but who request to stand on chairs or tables or add music and a dance routine. I enjoy being around people who ask for more spirit days or want to volunteer for more afterschool activities because they know the positive impact it has on their students. I love being around people who don't mind embarrassing themselves because they know their foolishness might make at least one student in their classroom step out of their comfort zone or crack a smile. I want to be around people who are "all in."

If you want to get an honest gauge of the climate and culture of your school, survey your students. I have learned throughout the years that sometimes adults just tell each other what they want to hear, but students … well, they'll be straight-up honest with you. Therefore, I encourage you to ask your students three simple questions:

1. Do you *have* to come to school or do you *want* to come to school?

2.   How do your teachers make you feel?

3.   Does your school community feel like a family?

The information you gather from these questions can be incredibly enlightening. Once you share this data with your leadership team, you can make more informed decisions on how to increase enthusiasm and community. You could decide to bring in a motivational speaker to improve your weaknesses. You could develop school activities or evening events to address the concerns. You could begin a school climate and culture professional learning committee or even purchase a book for each teacher about building a positive and enthusiastic school culture and climate. But I would suggest investing your time, money, and effort into implementing a new approach to your school spirit program.

The first two years that I was a principal at Greenwood Elementary School in Richmond, we implemented a program called Battle of the Classes, which divided each grade level into their own team. Each team had its own color, slogan, and chants that it performed at pep rallies and assemblies. Battle of the Classes rewarded points for the largest participation on spirit days and evening events such as a moonlight bike ride, parent field day, Father vs. Son Dodgeball Tournament, Book Camp Out, Ninja Obstacle Course, Bottle Cap Art Night, soccer tournament, board game night, Jedi Training, and the list goes on. Our school saw an immediate positive impact on the school's climate and culture by simply adding competition (and an enormous trophy for the grade with the most points at the end of the year).

Battle of the Classes decreased bullying, classroom discipline problems, suspensions, tardiness, and early dismissals. We saw huge gains in staff morale. Battle of the Classes was a simple event that made a significant impact; however, in December of 2017, our student survey results on our school climate and culture really opened my eyes. I noticed that our students were only developing relationships with students within their own classrooms. Many students wanted to mentor other students but did not have the opportunity. The seniors of our school, the fifth graders, even requested more leadership opportunities. Battle of the Classes was part of the solution, but not all of it. The rest came to me on

December 10, 2017 in Atlanta, Georgia, at a professional development conference at the Ron Clark Academy.

The Ron Clark Academy (RCA) is a nonprofit middle school for fifth through eighth graders. RCA has received recognition for its tremendous success in educating the *whole* child. Educators from across the globe visit this school annually to learn not only best practices in the classroom, but most importantly, how to engage and develop long-lasting relationships with their students. It has always been a dream of mine to visit this school, and for my birthday weekend, my school district made an item on my bucket list become a reality.

In trying to describe my experience at the Ron Clark Academy, words like "awesome" and "magical" come to mind, and they certainly fit, but the one word that best sums it up is "passion." I was almost unable to take in everything there was to see, hear, and learn at the RCA. Peering into colorful and spacious classrooms (all decked out with bright and colorful themes), I saw students standing on desks and teachers sitting on tables playing guitars. Some students had bongo drums at their desks. Music and laughter filled my ears as I floated through the building. Academic rigor is the norm, and behavioral expectations are high, but every student and staff member there is filled with so much passion for learning and excellence that it spills out over every inch of space that the academy occupies.

When I returned from my conference in Atlanta, I had extra pep in my step. I woke up even earlier than usual. I turned the music up even louder. I not only opened car doors for students, but I gave the parents high fives and hugs before they drove off. I changed the direction our bus riders entered the school building so I could see each child every morning before the two-week winter break.

In the classroom, I immediately implemented many of Clark's chants. I hopped from desk to desk while coteaching a difficult math concept with some of the amazing teachers at my school. Students smiled from ear to ear and matched my renewed enthusiasm by repeating my chants with equal energy. The teachers understood immediately that Ron Clark had made a huge impact in my life.

After my visit to Atlanta, I revised our Battle of the Classes program to include many of the attributes of the Ron Clark Academy spirit program. I wanted to build a culture of excellence through authentic connection using this system, one that did not stop at grade level. Therefore, our entire school of 700-plus students in kindergarten through fifth grade were mixed and split into five "houses." Houses were named after our five Gator Values: Gratitude, Accountability, Trustworthiness, Optimism, and Respect.

The purpose of the House System is to tear down any walls within our classroom family. It aims to give students an identity and sense of pride in a supportive, collaborative, and secure environment. This initiative provides positive competition and a closer rapport between students and teachers on multiple grade levels. Through the House System, each student is assigned a student mentor from another grade level who serves as a "buddy" that he or she connects with throughout the year. This provides our leaders more opportunities to let their light shine.

At Greenwood, our volunteer "spirit team" of teachers developed a house name, crest, slogan, fable, and chant for each house. This team developed a Google spreadsheet that's used by all staff members to give students points as a consistent incentive for classroom behavior, academic excellence, attendance, and participation in the total school program. We developed a website to display a graph that highlights each house's current total points. Our Student Council Association changed its name to the House Council, and three student leaders have been elected by each house (these worthy leaders received an old-school varsity jacket with their house crest at a candle lighting ceremony). The spirit team then worked with a custom art company to develop house shirts, scarves, hats, notebooks, socks, pencils, and tattoos for all participants.

Furthermore, our spirit team reached out to community businesses to secure financial sponsorships that took the house initiative to the next level of excellence. With local businesses sponsoring each house for $3,000, we were able to purchase a lighting system in the cafeteria that displays the color of the winning house. We purchased TVs for our cafeteria and hallway that display the total amount of points each house has received. We took each house to the YMCA for a quarterly pool party, and we hosted a monthly house breakfast for students and parents.

But getting 700 students initially split into four houses is a daunting task. At the Ron Clark Academy, students spun a huge wheel with the four houses on it, and I loved that concept. But for our first year of the House System at Greenwood, spinning a wheel 700 times could have taken five weeks. So the spirit team decided to purposefully assign students into houses for that first year, which worked out perfectly. For future participants, one of our teacher's husbands designed a house wheel, which we already use at pep rallies to welcome new students, teachers, community partners, bus drivers, cafeteria workers, and our custodial and maintenance team into a house.

The House System has virtually transformed our school in ways that I never could have predicted or dreamed. It provides a positive and consistent schoolwide behavioral system and has helped to dramatically increase student achievement—socially, emotionally, and academically. Our students are more intrinsically motivated, and they are learning how to become successful leaders who can motivate others. School attendance has improved, and tardiness and early dismissals have been significantly reduced. Since house members have to work together in order to succeed and win challenges, the students have had the chance to develop new friendships and gain civic awareness. Administrators from other schools have even visited our school to see the House System in action. Best of all, family and student engagement have both skyrocketed. We are many houses at Greenwood, but we are one big family. With every house event and pep rally, I can feel our family growing bigger and stronger—and that's what Lifeline 65 is all about.

Be Ready

Educators are never handed the same thing day after day. We all need to be ready for the inherent unpredictability that comes with working with students and coworkers in a school setting. In what ways can you ready yourself to meet and exceed the needs of your students? Are you ready to be adaptable and creative in your approach to building these relationships?

The greatest gift anyone can give a child is the gift of time. Whether you're spending time with your students at a sporting event, musical performance, art festival, community parade, bazaar, yard sale, outdoor garden, or silent auction, your students will be appreciative. The additional time you put into building authentic relationships with your students will make a significant impact on your students' academic performance, as well as their social and emotional learning.

The same goes for building relationships with parents and the community. Think creatively about how to stay connected with families over the weekend. I encourage your school to host a Father's Day two-on-two basketball tournament or a seniors versus parents powderpuff football game. Host a fall festival with live music, a scarecrow auction, pumpkin painting, bobbing for apples, and a parent dunk tank. Have a chili cook-off, bake sale, or even a tailgate party for the local college football team. Host a March Madness viewing party or a Saturday night Parents' Night Out.

I've even created programs for *future* students at my elementary school. For example, I created a six-week soccer program in the fall and a five-week basketball program in the winter for two- and three-year-old kids, because nothing in my area existed for these age groups. What started as only five kids in each program eventually became 25 with eight dads coaching. Do whatever you need to do to get families on your campus.

If trying to work with the parents of some students seems to hit a dead end, I have found great success in partnering with neighborhood recreation centers, YMCAs, Boys and Girls Clubs, churches, or day-care centers to reengage the family. I have also had success in taking the show "on the road": I hosted a basketball tournament and cookout *off* campus; I held a few back-to-school sessions in the community room of an apartment complex. I have met with parents and their children in their own living rooms on a Saturday afternoon. I have brought donuts and coffee for a Saturday morning Coffee Chat at a local gym. I have brought a projector with a large screen for a movie night and ordered an ice cream truck. I have been to a pool party, luau, and even a silent auction with a DJ on a Saturday evening. Another favorite has been dressing in costume with teacher friends and delivering pizzas as a school fundraiser. Do whatever is necessary to get families involved.

Engaged families impact student achievement dramatically, but the hardest part of family engagement is getting parents to take that first step inside the school doors. Some parents might have had a difficult school experience themselves. Some parents have to work two or three jobs and literally do not have the time. Some parents might be intimidated by the school. Some parents want to get involved but do not know how, other than donating money. Whatever the reasons may be, I can promise you that connecting with a child on a Saturday, or otherwise outside of school hours, can begin to break down those barriers. No matter the situation, be ready to make the extra effort to reach those seemingly out-of-reach parents. It will make a huge difference in their lives and contribute in countless ways to the life of your school.

In no way did I feel ready to face María at the basketball game after her fish was shredded to smithereens. But I was ready and willing to offer my presence, and I hoped that showing up was going to be enough. As it turned out, it most definitely was. My old friends Mr. Decrosta, Ms. Westhead, and Coach Rhoades were willing to show up in the classroom or gym early on a Monday morning for me and students like me. In their wisdom, they knew the importance of being ready. They were ready to meet a child like me, right where I was. They were ready to listen and remain interested in what I had to say, they were ready to sacrifice some of their 65 weekend hours for me and for many others in order to reduce our time away from school. They believed in Lifeline 65 before it had a name.

"If a child is to keep alive his inborn sense of wonder without any such gift from the fairies, he needs the companionship of at least one adult who can share it, rediscovering with him the joy, excitement, and mystery of the world we live in."

—*Rachel Carson*

Sunday

Bryan

"Get to know me."

S unday. A day to sleep in. Catch up on *This is Us* on NBC. Fire up the Big Green Egg and marinate a Boston butt for an eight-hour smoke. Blast Lionel Richie's "Easy Like Sunday Morning" on repeat while taking a long, invigorating shower to start the day. Throw on a favorite football jersey and enjoy a Bloody Mary at the breakfast table with friends while discussing plans for the rest of your "Sunday Funday." Visit a brewery for lunch. Take a nap from two to four. Devour at least 20 garlic and parmesan wings while watching Tom Brady dominate the turf. Take a second relaxing shower, ease into some laundry-fresh pj's, and climb into bed to watch *Game of Thrones* on HBO as you nod off to sleep.

Yeah, that Sunday sounds dreamy alright, because it does not describe the reality of my Sundays at all. My Sundays are made up of sunrise Katy Perry and Calvin Harris dance parties with my four-year-old son and three-year-old daughter. I play the same shows over and over on Disney Junior while I make waffles for my daughter and pancakes for my son and brew at least 18 cups of coffee for the two tired adults in the house. Around six o'clock, I usually attempt to take a peaceful shower, but anyone with young kids knows that the bathroom is a community space where community affairs occur, and privacy has no meaning. Therefore, I rush through my morning shower at breakneck speed while both children bang on the glass door. The whole unseemly process lasts two minutes. Then, my son picks out my outfit while my wife attempts to wrangle everyone toward the breakfast table. It's a miracle if breakfast lasts longer than four minutes and 20 seconds before complete chaos breaks out. I'm forced to merely fantasize about brewery visits with friends as I cut the grass, fold the laundry, and pick up about 200 toys before nine in the morning. I wish I could give my full attention to Sunday School lessons instead of thinking about the 500 report cards waiting for me at home to review. To tell the truth, most Sundays we eat frozen dinosaur-shaped chicken nuggets for lunch, and definitely not a smoked Boston Butt. One day I'll have the stamina to stay up past nine on a Sunday evening so I can watch *Game of Thrones*, but for now I usually end up humming "Let it Go" with my kids as I fall asleep. The future is bright, but in the meantime, I will continue to enjoy and appreciate every day that I am given as my children grow up right before my eyes at a scary rate. Sunday is a great day to hang out and do fun things with the people you care about. Sometimes this means visits to the park with our children or maybe a day trip to the mountains. Sometimes I use a Sunday afternoon to connect with my students and build more meaningful and authentic relationships.

As a teacher, I started each year by giving my students a "Get to Know Me" activity sheet. This way I could find out how my students learned best, what subjects they enjoyed the most, and what exactly they'd already heard about their new teacher, Mr. Stein. But it was really their interests and hobbies I was hunting for. So I put a question on the sheet that read, "If Mr. Stein could attend an activity with you outside of school, what would it be?" I got all types of responses: realistic ones like attending church, soccer games, karate practice, dance recitals, birthday parties, Rubik's Cube team competitions, or Chuck E. Cheese's; and unrealistic ones like flying to Disneyland or driving two hours east for a day at the beach. Using this information, I contacted each child's parents to explain my plans of connecting with their family on a Sunday that worked best for them. It took some effort, but in comparing schedules, I was often able to attend games and competitions that several of my students participated in together and at the same time.

I really enjoyed attending these events outside of school. In my nine years as a classroom teacher, I was privileged to see my students do some pretty cool things. I was there to see a basketball win at the buzzer, listened to a beautiful vocal solo in front of an enormous crowd, and witnessed the pride and satisfaction of a student advancing his Boy

Scout rank. As enthusiastic as my students and parents were about my Sunday visits, sometimes my presence would make my students very nervous, and they would not perform well on the athletic field. One afternoon, I was politely asked to leave the baseball field as one mother's son was zero-for-four from the plate in a heated playoff battle.

For some students that did not, or could not, participate in weekend activities, I hosted a variety of competitions at my school on Sunday afternoons, which included Math 24, Destination Imagination, and robotics. Some of these activities went well, and others were a one-and-done experience. Some Sundays, I just sent an open invitation for a playground playdate for an hour. It was all worth the effort. My students understood that I truly cared about them, and they appreciated the chance to participate. It also made calling parents so much easier if I had a situation to discuss, because they saw firsthand that I was willing to invest in their children.

I also believe that attending coworkers' events makes work a happier and more efficient environment. In 2015 alone, I attended more baby and wedding showers than all of my nonteaching friends will attend over the course of their lives. One weekend, a member of the maintenance team at my school invited me to see him play the drums at his church. I arrived at eight in the morning and the service did not end until after two that afternoon. I had a difficult time explaining to my wife that I was not having a Sunday Funday at a brewery but was instead standing, clapping, and jamming for six hours of spirited worship.

Out of all the events I've attended over the years, none stick out more than Bryan's basketball game. Bryan was a high school junior when I first met him. I was the head varsity basketball coach at Glen Allen High School in Virginia, and even though Bryan tried out and did not make the team, our coaching staff decided to keep him as our student manager because we all saw something special in him. Bryan has a charismatic and vivacious personality and is part of a stellar family. He loves to dance, sing, and play basketball. He makes others smile. Bryan's greatest gift is that he has the ability to make the people around him better just by offering his support and enthusiasm to everyone he encounters.

During our Glen Allen High School basketball games, Bryan cheered his heart out. He enjoyed yelling at the referees and giving high fives to his teammates when they subbed out of the game. During timeouts, Bryan often forgot to bring water to our players because he was dancing with the pep band, and the crowd loved it. In the locker room, Bryan liked to repeat everything I said to the team. And since I could get heated at times (especially if our team was losing at half-time), another coach would stay in the hallway with Bryan, where he was safely out of earshot from my salty locker room talk. Bryan kept meticulous tabs on the NBA, and his attention to detail, coupled with his ability to remember so many stats, always amazed me. Bryan would bolt in my direction in the school hallways and the grocery store to tell me if the Chicago Bulls had won their last game or not.

While he did not play on our high school team, Bryan did play on another basketball team that was part of the organization Jacob's Chance. Jacob's Chance is a nonprofit in the Richmond area that provides team-oriented competitive opportunities for students with special needs of all ages. Therefore, when Bryan asked me to attend one of his games on a Sunday afternoon, I did not hesitate one second to go and see him in action.

When I walked into the gym, I was blown away. There were volunteers of all ages helping the athletes dribble, pass, and shoot the basketball. Parents cheered on the sidelines every time a basket was made. The athletes' smiles were priceless. Out of all the basketball games I have been to in my life, this was by far the best.

On the court, it was easy to spot Bryan. Not only was he the tallest player on his team, but he also took it upon himself to keep things running smoothly and fairly by telling the volunteers and his teammates whose turn it was to dribble and shoot the ball. Bryan hustled up and down the court and grabbed a ton of rebounds. He cheered on his teammates and reminded the scorekeepers to add two points every time a bucket was made. He never missed a thing. Bryan didn't mind sharing the ball, but he loved shooting and scoring points. Watching his face light up each time he did this was definitely worth the price of admission.

Just like the many other students I visited on Sundays, Bryan and I became even closer after I went to see his game. We stayed in touch after our season, and when his senior year arrived, our coaching staff wanted Bryan to play in front of the entire school at the winter sports pep rally. Nobody really cared about our star basketball player dunking the ball, or the hype video I spent 10 hours creating for the event, but when Bryan scored six points in front of over 1,000 people, the place erupted after each basket. At the end of the season, our coaching staff decided to create an award and name it after Bryan. This recognition is given each year to a selfless teammate who lives out our team's values and demonstrates a love for their teammates, the school, and basketball. In fact, at his high school graduation ceremony, Bryan's 2,000-plus classmates voted him "Mr. Glen Allen High School" because nobody loved being a Jaguar more than Bryan.

After Bryan graduated, I made the tough decision to move out of the classroom and into administration at a new school. My goal was to impact as many lives as possible, and I thought as a principal, I would be able to connect with many more students, teachers, and families. The toughest part about making this move was that I had to give up coaching, which I still miss to this day. But at my new school, when our librarian was looking for a detail-oriented and spirited volunteer to assist with filing books, I knew exactly who to call.

Over the years, my friendship with Bryan has continued to grow. Now I look forward to seeing him every Thursday when he stops by my office on the way to the library to give me the inside scoop on the Chicago Bulls. We often meet up at college sporting events, and I was honored to see him sing at his church. And I still get to see him in action on the basketball court, because his team now calls Greenwood their home court. Our school even did a fundraiser to purchase new uniforms for the Jacob's Chance organization. On the court and off, Bryan continues to make people around him better. I hope that he will always be a part of my life.

I would trade sleep, Netflix, grilling, private showers, and any other Sunday Funday activity for the chance to build strong, lasting relationships with my students. I fully understand that visiting students outside of school time can be a tough task, and I struggled each year to make it to all of my students' activities. Sundays can be especially tricky to navigate because of church commitments and family time. But with some creativity and ingenuity, this can be an ideal day on which to make incomparable, lasting connections. I can promise you, the time I took to do this made a huge impact on me and opened my eyes to more than I could have imagined. My Sunday connections made me realize that time is the greatest gift an educator can give to his students. I believe that in order to reach the highest levels of success, one must be willing to make great sacrifices.

Most importantly, my Sunday connections taught me that if the world had more people like Bryan in it, there would be a lot more smiling, singing, and dancing.

Carpool

As a teacher, I was limited in regard to the number of field trips I was allowed to take each school year with my students. Distance restrictions and funding limitations made going off campus even more difficult. Therefore, if I read a historical fiction novel with my students and then wanted to visit a Civil War battlefield referenced in the book, it might not happen. But when I discovered that many places I wanted to visit with my class did not charge admission on Sundays, the solution to this problem was simple: Sunday carpool!

Once each marking period, a group of volunteer parents and I would pile my class into our cars and take a special field trip. We visited Saint John's Church to see a reenactment of Patrick Henry's famous "Give Me Liberty or Give Me Death" speech. We traveled to Petersburg, Virginia, to see the battlefield and historical artifacts that were mentioned in Carolyn Reeder's novel, *Across the Lines*. We drove to Jamestown, Pamplin Park, Henricus Park, Williamsburg, Monticello, and even Mount Vernon. All of these field trips normally would have cost our students a fortune, but special arrangements made them free.

Our basketball team also took several carpool field trips on Sundays. I made it a point to take the team on a college visit and campus tour each year. If one of our seniors was participating in an internship, we carpooled to his work so the younger players could see that academic excellence was a top priority. We genuinely enjoyed each other's company and accomplished a variety of things together, for our own benefit and for the benefit of others. We hosted a Sunday basketball clinic for elementary school students, planted trees and flowers in the school garden area, and ran and laughed our way through powdery puffs of color in the "Color Me Rad" Fun Run. We didn't laugh as much during our five-in-the-morning Sunday Seal Team workouts, but we still managed to have fun. Since food is one of my favorite things, it may surprise no one that I especially enjoyed the cooking class we took together and the Sunday dinners that we shared from time to time.

If you were to ask my students and basketball players the best part about these Sunday field trips, I can guarantee they would all say the road trip. Being in the car for several hours allowed us to have real life conversations like Mr. DeCrosta, Ms. Westhead, and Coach Rhoades used to have with me. A conversation that I'll always remember is one I had with our senior captain on one of these road trips.

TJ had played basketball during his entire high school career, and his family was not terribly involved in his life. TJ was anxious about our upcoming senior night, concerned that there would be no one to walk him out onto the court. It made me realize how difficult this night would be for a number of my players who had little parental support. After our trip, I took it upon myself to visit TJ's mom at home to let her know how much I loved her son and to let her know that I hoped she would make it to at least one game this year, especially senior night. Well, TJ's mom did show up for senior night, and she was there to walk him out onto the court when his name was announced. Cheers erupted as TJ walked proudly to the middle of the gym, with his mother beaming on his arm. During the game that night, TJ dominated. He led us to the win and the regular season conference championship title. It was the only game in four years that TJ's mom attended, but at least she was there for the most important one. Appearing uninvited at TJ's home, when I had never met his family, in order to have a very real conversation, was not an easy thing to do; however, I'd do it again and again if that's what it takes to get otherwise disengaged parents to be present for their children. I have found that when I invest enough time in my students, to the point that I am able to be real and build authentic relationships with them and their families, I earn their trust and build a sense of safety that allows me to take more risks in the classroom.

Sunday Communication

During the summer, I would purchase three dozen thank you cards in green and three dozen more in blue. This gave me a total of 72 thank you cards, which I bought at the Dollar Store for six dollars total. Every Sunday, starting at the beginning of the schoolyear, I took one thank you card from each stack and wrote a handwritten note.

Each green thank you card went to a child. This child could be in my class or on my basketball team. Sometimes, if I saw a student from another class complete an amazing project or assist a friend in the hallway, I would write that child a thank you card. I also used my green pile for the student teachers and high school volunteers who assisted in my classroom each year. Each blue card went to a central office administrator, community partner, or parent. I am a strong believer in developing positive relationships with all stakeholders in the school community, and a simple, handwritten thank you card really goes a long way.

As an administrator, I use Sunday as a day to communicate all the exciting events taking place over the upcoming week. At six o'clock every Sunday evening, I send a voice message, email, and text to all families and school staff. A dream of mine is to one day use that voicemail to announce a student who wins a special ride to school the following morning in a limo or a car decorated as a gator (our mascot). If I can't pull that off, how cool would it be if this lucky student got to ride to school with the principal and our mascot in the principal's car?

On Sundays I use the power of social media to post pictures and videos that will get the students excited for school on Monday. Right before Thanksgiving last year, I shared a video on our school's Facebook page about the 30 hidden paper turkeys that had been stashed all over the building, waiting to be found. This was a simple and easy thing to do, but it seemed to generate a ton of anticipation and excitement among the students and staff. In order to drive up attendance for our staff basketball game last year, I created a hype video featuring our star faculty athletes, and it did the trick—our charity event basketball game was standing-room only.

Posting about the unique things happening at your school absolutely bridges the gap between the school and its families and is more and more becoming an integral part of ensuring the Lifeline 65 philosophy. And if I can manage to get my children down for a quick hour nap, I make a positive phone call to one to three students to tell them and their family how much I appreciate them and their contributions to our school community.

Expressing our gratitude, even in the simplest ways, opens our minds and hearts so that we may be ready for what life has in store for us. Don't miss out on the chance to say "thank you" for something each and every day.

"Gratitude makes sense of our past, brings peace for today, and creates a vision for tomorrow."

—*Melody Beattie*

Stein Time Bank

Imagine this: you post a chart in the front of the classroom with a section for each letter grade—A's at the top, F's at the bottom, and everything else in between. Each student receives a clip with his or her name on it, and throughout the year when a child takes a test, completes a project, or forgets to turn in homework, the name clip moves up or down. This way, every student can keep an eye on how they're doing academically at any moment—and so can the rest of the class.

I don't know about your school, but I know that if my school implemented this system for grades, 600-plus parents would be in the main office first thing in the morning. But I don't see much of a difference between the system I described above and the behavior management system used in so many classrooms at the elementary school level. How many teachers in your building are currently using a clip chart system? If you are, please toss that system away ASAP and develop a behavior management plan with real-life implications.

In my classroom, I implemented Stein Time Bank. This was a system in which my students received 200 dollars in colored marbles each Monday for coming to "work" and doing their best. Throughout the week, the students could receive more money by doing extraordinary deeds like helping a friend, cleaning up in the cafeteria, picking up the playground equipment, improving their math grade, reading an extra 15 minutes for homework, and the list goes on and on. On the flip side, students could lose money for using profanity, stealing, cutting in line, forgetting their homework, and other poor decisions. Students also had to pay me 15 dollars in "rent" every Friday for their weekly access to the classroom lights, desks, pencil sharpener, air conditioner, and heat.

Every other week, our classroom hosted a two-minute flea market. Students were allowed to bring one item from home and sell it to a classmate. Some students would just save their money and not purchase any items. Some students used all their money to buy ten items. I even had one student who bought as many items as he could and then resold them at a higher rate.

As the students accumulated a lot of marbles and their money pouches became full, I taught them how to invest their money. As a third-grade teacher, I taught my class about savings accounts and investing in a bank with the highest interest rates. As a fourth-grade teacher, I taught them about managing checking accounts and buying "real estate," aka the desks and tables in our classroom. My students truly loved collecting weekly rent checks from their peers. As a fifth-grade teacher, I took Stein Time Bank to a more rigorous level as my students were divided into groups and instructed to develop their own businesses. Each group would create a business website, business cards, marketing materials, and commercials. Finally, I taught my class about stocks and how to invest in each other's companies. The stock value of each group would go up and down according to their behavior. The most amazing part about this particular project was that each year, I'd put my most behaviorally challenged students in the same group and, nine out of 10 times, their business was the most successful.

In addition to fiscal management, our Stein Time Bank activities taught my students the importance of giving back to the community. Our class created a list of three to five nonprofits to which students could donate their "money": the Richmond SPCA, the American Cancer Society, and FeedMore (our local food bank), were some of the most popular recipients. Some students donated to their nonprofits weekly and some donated monthly, but they all did so with a great deal of pride. This special aspect of Stein Time Bank created a spirit of generosity that filled our classroom and hopefully had a lasting effect on my students.

Of all the facets of Stein Time Bank, the part I enjoyed most came every Sunday. Students could receive an extra 50 dollars on Monday morning if they posted a short story describing how they helped someone over the weekend. Most of the time, my students wrote about their siblings or parents, but sometimes I got a great story about helping a teammate on a sports team, neighbors needing assistance, or a member at church who needed a friend. These stories would lead to great conversations for our Monday morning meetings.

I would also offer 50 dollars for completing my weekend challenge, which included Sudoku, Word Boggle Board, or even a list of house chores to complete. Once a month, students could earn 100 dollars for participating in my 15-minute online study session using TodaysMeet (a phone app) on a Sunday afternoon. Although only 60 percent of my students had a computer at home, over 90 percent had internet on their cell phone, which led to almost 100 percent of my students completing this voluntary task on a Sunday! Finally, I offered my students 100 dollars to attend a classmate's sporting event over the weekend, which led to some wonderful and unexpected stories and connections.

The Stein Time Bank became so much more than a plan to incentivize desired behavior within our classroom family. It connected students outside of school hours, and in ways that they never would have connected otherwise. Beyond the opportunities I created, the children and families ended up arranging play dates and get-togethers with each other all on their own. And because the children were learning about fiscal responsibility, they grew more empathetic and appreciative of their parents, and thankful for what they had. Our classroom family, and the families of my students, were impacted in so many positive ways, and that meant the world to all of us.

"Family is not an important thing. It's everything."
—*Michael J. Fox*

Superhero

Have you ever heard of Bubba? No? Well, he's orange with three white bands outlined in black on his head and body, and he's about four inches long. Still no? He has a rounded tail and his dorsal fin is lined with stripes. He used to live in a coral reef on the coast of Australia. Not ringing any bells yet? I'm not really surprised. You see, Bubba is Nemo's forgotten cousin. While moviegoers everywhere became obsessed with helping Dory and Marlin find adventurous little Nemo, no one ever really thought about Bubba.

Bubba longed for adventures even greater than those of Nemo. So after Bubba made his way to America and into my classroom one year, my students took turns taking Bubba home, in order to provide him with the life of excitement he craved. Bubba, a plush clownfish stuffed animal, quickly became part of all of our families. Who doesn't love a clownfish who's ready to roll on a moment's notice? The students wrote stories and took pictures of their exciting weekend adventures with him. Bubba rode on rollercoasters at Kings Dominion. He sat in a movie theater and saw Mary Poppins on Broadway. He went down slides at many different parks. Bubba rode trains and planes and lounged on a Disney cruise ship. He went on class field trips and rode around the track in a stroller for our Saturday morning running club. He attended multiple sporting events, a Daddy-Daughter Dance, and several PTA meetings. He went to the mall, restaurants, Starbucks, Build-a-Bear, and even Great Clips for a haircut. Towards the end of the school year, I published all of the students' stories and pictures into beautiful Bubba memory books for each of them.

The most fun part of this project each year was when I got to come up with the character (it wasn't always Bubba) and the backstory for its reason to travel from house to house. I have used the genie from *Aladdin*, Sebastian the crab from *The Little Mermaid*, and other colorful stuffed animals. I always tried to pair our mascot with the current class interest, so I did not decide who our class friend would be until after the first month of school.

One year, my classroom was full of students with a strong interest in the Marvel comics, as new Avenger movies were popping out left and right. Students wore Captain America shirts and Iron Man pants and carried Hulk lunch boxes to the cafeteria. I couldn't shake these characters, so instead of adopting a stuffed classroom mascot that year, I decided to have my students turn themselves into superheroes of their own creation. Instead of having them write a weekend story just once throughout the year, the students kept a year-long weekend journal of all their adventures. They had to create their own costumes and write about their powers in great detail. They took pictures of their superhero selves as they carried out good deeds and completed incredible missions throughout the year. I also strongly encouraged the students to join forces with other students in the class at least one time that year to solve a major problem. This led to many play dates among my students, which made our classroom family even stronger.

There's no question that the highlight of this particular year for me was that I, too, created my own superhero. His name is Captain Chicken Feet, and he is the world's fastest and most powerful chicken. Like MacGyver, Captain Chicken Feet uses his intellect to create useful superhero-type gadgets out of anything. The students recruited Captain Chicken Feet on several Sunday afternoons in order to collaborate and take down our nemeses. I guarantee that I had more fun with this particular project than the students did.

Be Present

This past year at our back-to-school night, I asked a representative from each student's family (a parent, grandparent, aunt, uncle, or guardian) to select a number from one to 28. I invited them to write that number down and tell their neighbor the number they selected (to keep them honest). I then asked the families to stand as quickly as they could when I shouted their number. Sometimes I even instructed them to make different animal sounds, complete a chant, or dance. It was always fun and got a lot of laughs. But I ended this activity by stating the following:

Please stand if you selected a number between one and 28. That number represents a day that happens each month. There are 12 months in the year. Therefore, you have 12 opportunities this year to give *time* to your child and our school on that day. If you selected the number 15, you can volunteer on January 15th, February 15th, March 15th, and so on. You can volunteer on all twelve dates if you want. But all we are asking is that you remain true to your date at least once this year. We are not asking for donations. We are simply asking for your time to build relationships within these walls and to become a part of our school family. As Rick Warren stated, "The best way to spell relationship is T-I-M-E."

I have found that Sundays are a great day for families to give time to the school in all kinds of ways. I have had families string up lights in the trees to provide a more welcoming feeling during the winter holidays. Parents and students wrote inspirational messages in sidewalk chalk during the state testing season. "Fat heads" (life-sized photos turned into wall decals) of the teachers were posted in the front of the school during teacher appreciation week. Large signs of appreciation were designed and posted the Sunday evening before bus driver appreciation week. One year, parents even set up an obstacle course for our student bus riders to complete as they entered the building on Monday morning. I'll be honest, it was a little hectic on the bus ramp, but the time given up on a Sunday to create this exciting experience set the tone for another magical week at school.

Sunday is a great day to bring the community together. Planning even just one Sunday event in a year could make a huge impact on achieving your school's goals. My only advice is whatever event you choose, be present. If you choose to host a family picnic, silent auction, football tailgate party, Easter egg hunt, casino night, or one-mile pet run on your campus, be present. If you take your community off campus for a tacky light tour, bowling outing, Sunday movie night, ice skating, or an incredible fishing and canoe adventure, be present.

I have found that families with a student with special needs can really struggle to schedule playdates with other students. Their parents sometimes don't know how to have this conversation with other families or how to get the ball rolling on behalf of their child. You could schedule a monthly playground date at your school if you have special needs programs and help bridge this gap. Help in whatever ways that you can to create friendship opportunities for all of your students.

Be present for the people in your life and give them your time. Whether that's by attending a sporting event, an academic competition, or a dance recital, relationships are built by being *present*. I would not have the relationship I have with Bryan if I did not make the time. With only 24 hours in a day, some sacrifices have to be made, and typically it's time watching television, doing chores, or hanging with friends and family. Sacrifices are necessary to make a huge impact, but priorities and personal values should never be compromised. I am grateful every single day that my mentors were able and willing to be present for me. Being present means exactly that. Be involved. Cheer. Connect with families. Have real conversations, even when it's hard. High five. Put down the phone. Enjoy.

"The best and most beautiful things in the world cannot be seen or even touched. They must be felt with the heart."

—*Helen Keller*

Holiday Breaks

Holly

"Don't stop believin'"
Hold on ____ ____ ____."

"Now this is a story all about how
My life got flipped-turned____ ____."

Most of you were probably able to jam out the lyrics to those classic songs. Our ability to retain useless (albeit fun) information seems limitless, but our memories can sometimes fail us in a clutch. How is it that I can remember the lyrics to these songs from many years ago, yet I struggle to remember what items to pick up at the grocery store? It seems memory, along with the brain's mechanisms for learning, are funny and often capricious things.

As a classroom teacher, I was always searching for innovative ways to help my students learn and remember social studies content, especially over holiday breaks. I tried traditional means like study guides, note cards, and notebooks, and some more contemporary methods such as interactive notebooks, flipbooks, bright and colorful posters, foldables, and even online study chats I wanted my students to stay sharp while they spent time away from school because I found that many of my students would forget much of the information I'd taught prior to the break. It wasn't until I met a student named Holly that I found a solution to this problem.

Holly was a dreamer who dreamed *big*. She always took the lead and went all the way over the top when it came to group projects. If Holly was given the option to complete one of three book report projects, she would enjoy completing all three. She was the president of the book club, newspaper, and SCA. She loved music and art. With her independent classwork, she was a perfectionist and extremely detail-oriented. Holly was one of those students who would remind me when we had to go to lunch or when I had to alter our schedule because of an assembly later on in the day. Holly is the only student who ever used stickies to remind me of important tasks I needed to complete throughout the week. No joke! I am convinced that Holly will be the CEO of a Fortune 500 company in the near future.

Holly took great pride in her grades and, at times, put a lot of pressure on herself. Because Holly was consistently such a model student, it was quickly apparent to me that she had a hard time retaining information whenever we had a break from school that lasted longer than a normal weekend. Holly primarily struggled with social studies content, and her grade faltered after winter break. Since Holly was basically like my personal secretary, I really wanted to do something to help her succeed. Holly loved music, so one evening, I decided to record a rap song about the abolitionist movement using GarageBand on my Mac computer. I included all the vocabulary words, important dates, battles, and influential abolitionists we needed to learn. The next morning, I invited another classmate, Connor, to stay with me during lunch to record the hook, and by dismissal, my special gift for Holly was ready.

When I gave Holly my present, her eyes lit up, and she demanded that I play the song for the entire class. Now, to say that I am not a talented rapper or singer is putting it mildly. In fact, what I did on that track was not really rapping or singing—it was more like a new genre, called the "Enthusiastically Speaking Over Musical Beats" genre—so I was more than a little nervous to hear the students' reactions. But I put the CD in the music player, turned the volume all the way up, and hit play.

The kids loved it. They were dancing all over the room. They demanded that I provide them with copies of the lyrics to memorize the song, and each child wanted his own copy. I hurried to Best Buy to purchase 50 blank CDs. Within three days, the students had the song, which contained all of the content from the abolitionist unit, completely memorized. As a result, our class crushed the end of unit "celebration" (test). This song was even shuffled into the mix for our Friday dance parties, at the request of my students.

By the end of the week, I received a handwritten thank you card from Holly that read:

> Mr. Stein,
>
> Thank you for the CD. You know that Connor singing on the song is the only reason why the students enjoy it. Just kidding. I hope you continue to make more songs.
>
> — Holly

Holly was right! I needed to make more songs, and that's exactly what I did. I had so much fun writing and recording two more songs on my home computer. Even though I am sure my students' parents were sick of hearing this new music genre in the evenings, their children were performing well in the classroom. As a matter of fact, our class's performance on the end-of-the-year state assessment was so outstanding that I was nominated and awarded the R.E.B. Award for Teaching Excellence from the Community Foundation. This award included a $13,000 grant that provided me with the opportunity to travel to Atlanta, Georgia, to pair up with my college roommate and music producer, Brandon Scott, to professionally record a history music album.

Producing this album over the summer is one of the highlights of my life, but I never could have imagined how much time and effort went into professionally recording a single song in a studio. Brandon Scott was the mastermind behind the entire operation, producing the beats and recruiting some incredibly talented singers to make our songs come alive. There were times that we'd stay up for three days in a row perfecting our project. After studio fees, mixing, and production costs, the $13,000 grant barely covered 20 percent of the total cost of this collaboration. I ended up digging into my own pockets, because I believed these songs could help many students just like Holly all over Virginia.

After a long summer, 20 songs were created in an album titled *Ryan Stein Presents History MVP*. I was so excited to implement all of it into my classroom and see the results in terms of my students' performance. From the very beginning of the year, the students memorized the songs that contained all the content, and unit after unit their scores soared.

Even after extended breaks, students came back knowing *more* information. While I was blown away and impressed by how well the songs worked, I remain truly grateful for the fact that I had the opportunity to reach so many students through this endeavor.

The next summer, I decided to take the album *Ryan Stein Presents History MVP* to another level. Not only would I produce thousands of hard copies of the album, but I also worked to get it onto iTunes, Spotify, and other music platforms so that students outside of my school would have access to this supplemental learning resource. Then I reached out to a literacy company to pair books and 21st century resources to this historical experience. I wanted to meet the needs of visual, auditory, and kinesthetic learners. It was my hope that the books and music would deepen their knowledge, as students gained confidence and developed an enthusiasm and, ultimately, a love for history.

Within the first two months of releasing this new comprehensive package, *History MVP* exploded and started to make an impact on children throughout Virginia. I attended conferences, where I got to share my story about Holly and her influence on creating this innovative tool. As its popularity spread throughout the state, *History MVP* provided me with the opportunity to conduct workshops at a variety of school districts and colleges and meet many amazing teachers and principals, and I will be forever grateful.

The year after I had Holly, I was lucky enough to be nominated by a group of parents as a Virginia Super Teacher, a distinction that recognizes the top six educators in Virginia. On a Friday afternoon, at our state testing pep rally, I was given this prestigious award and surprised with a $2,000 check from the Virginia Lottery. That same year, I was recognized as a top five national educator and had the opportunity to receive a teacher makeover from Jones of New York and meet Rachael Ray on national TV. All of these recognitions were simply amazing, and I'll always be thankful for the students, families, and friends who nominated me.

Long after Holly had moved on from my classroom, she still managed to keep tabs on me. She would even float me notes from time to time, like the one below. I'll never forget Holly, and whenever I think of her, I can't help but hear a little rap music playing in the back of my mind. If you're lucky enough to end up with a Holly in your class, don't hesitate to turn up the bass and let the learning flow. (No musical experience required, trust me.)

Mr. Stein,

You did a great job on the Rachael Ray show, but why were you swaying left to right on the stage like you had to poop? Just kidding :-) Keep impacting lives. You made a huge difference in mine. Thank you.

– Holly

PS: Remember it's your brother's birthday next week.

Picture Perfect

School personnel are always looking for innovative ideas for the bulletin boards near the main entrance of the school. I have seen Wall[s] of Excellence with perpetual plaques recognizing recipients of the teacher of the year, new teacher of the year, PTA volunteer of the year, and Battle of the Classes champions, which is wonderful. Schools may also consider posting pictures of their staff and students in black and white with powerful motivational quotes. I have seen bulletin boards filled with postcards from students' family members who live in other states or countries, and I think this is an excellent way to highlight school diversity.

The front of the building is also a great place to prominently display community partnerships. Include pictures of your community service projects, and visually keep track of how much money and time your staff and students are giving back to the community. Highlight major donors and, most importantly, what their contributions have done to benefit the student body. Pictures are powerful, and corporate America tends to be more willing to assist financially when they see the what their donated money provides.

I also encourage you to use highly visible bulletin boards to showcase collaborative projects. At our school, the kindergarten students did an amazing green-screen project with eighth graders, so we made sure to display their final projects. Our fourth- and fifth-grade drumline paired up with our local high school pep band, so we shared their efforts as well. We ran a camp and utilized middle school and high school volunteers, so we posted pictures of these volunteers working with our elementary school students. Use these bulletin boards to proudly bring attention to the magic that transpires between your school and the community.

Another bulletin board idea is called the traveling school flag. In the beginning of the school year, give each class two small "school flags." These could be simple little garden flags with your school mascot and mission statement on them. Throughout the year, as students travel to different locations with their class, they take and print pictures to post on the bulletin board. Students can even request to take a school flag over the holiday break if they are visiting a special historical location or traveling outside the country. Parents can post their child's picture on our school's social media platforms, and we can print it from there. By the end of the school year, you'll have a beautiful collage of pictures.

Finally, I would recommend keeping a personal binder, envelope, or scrapbook to keep some "picture perfect" moments you can revisit on a day that you need a laugh. Over the past 14 years, I have enjoyed printing hard copies of so many unforgettable moments. Revisiting these photos often helped motivate me in times when I felt overwhelmed or undeserving.

During my first year as a teacher, it started to snow so hard outside that I knew school would be closing early (people in the South tend to panic at the mere mention of snow). So I took my entire class outside and we had an epic flag football game in the snow. I can still hear the sounds of joy from my students. But 20 minutes later, the principal came on the loud speaker and announced that there would be no early dismissal. Our class went back inside to finish the day completely soaked and freezing, but we had the best experience and the biggest smiles when I snapped a class photo. Camera, *click*.

One day I jumped on a student's desk because I was so excited that he had answered a question correctly. In doing so, I split my pants. The class exploded in laughter. I was the only male teacher at the school and ended up having to wear one of my costumes the rest of the school day, which happened to be a homemade scarecrow. I had no other choice but to smile with the students and take a picture with the entire class. Camera, *click*.

One year, I decided to go sledding with some of my coworkers. The teachers selected a large hill that, unbeknownst to us, happened to be on a horse farm. We careened down the hill, laughing, as our lungs filled with the brisk country air. Once we tumbled off our sleds to run back up the hill, we smelled it before we saw it: we were covered in horse poop from head to toe. Camera, *click*.

Another year at a school with an outdoor campus, I was teaching a lesson when, suddenly, I heard loud screams of panic and cries for help coming from the classroom directly behind me. I quickly ran outside and beelined to the next building to assist. As I came around the corner, I saw it: a large buck had gotten his antlers stuck in one of the windows of the classroom. Even on an outdoor campus, no one had ever seen a deer in the neighborhood. As the buck violently thrashed his head in the glass and the principal called animal control, I did what any hero would do: I took out my phone. Camera, *click*.

Photographs speak a universal language and can bring people together in powerful ways. Use pictures to tell your story on social media, your school website, or blogs. By sharing yourself and your classroom in this way, you make yourself approachable and more "real" to those who view them. By highlighting successful and innovative lessons using photographs, you may just inspire some colleagues exactly when they need it most.

Photographs are evocative and can be used in a myriad of ways in the classroom. You can learn a great deal about your students by asking them what they believe is happening in a photo or how it makes them feel. A dog running toward the camera could be perceived as friend or foe. From there, you have a writing prompt that the children are excited about, because their responses to the photograph are unique to each of them, and their writings will be, too. By hanging photos of your students learning and having fun together inside your classroom, you'll foster a sense of comradery and build a more cohesive community of learners. The possibilities are nearly endless.

Napkin Notes

Holiday breaks are a great time to get community organizations involved with your school. I have connected with our local Boy and Girl Scout troops to provide canned food with handwritten inspirational notes on each bag. We've paired with churches to put hundreds of meals for families in Ziploc bags full of breakfast, lunch, and dinner. Target, Walmart, and local businesses have supplied coats, gloves, hats, sweatshirts, sweatpants, snow boots, and wool socks, and our school printed a special message to go with each item. Patient First, KidMed, and some local doctors have provided a care package for the winter cold and flu season. We've connected with local grocery stores to donate a Crock-Pot, microwave, or toaster to families in need. Nonprofit organizations have put together care packages including shampoo, soap, toothpaste, mouthwash, and other toiletry items. I am so grateful for our community partners.

Holiday breaks can be a special time to give your students a simple gift with a major impact. I have printed a picture of each of my students and written on the back, "I believe in you." I have made friendship bracelets. I have written personalized notes on popcorn bags for a family movie night and personalized water bottles with an inspirational message. After I created *Ryan Stein Presents History MVP*, I even gave everyone in the fourth grade a free CD. But after all that, one of the greatest holiday gifts that I've ever given to a student was a napkin note.

This idea came to me after reading *Napkin Notes* by Garth Callaghan. Garth was a father who wrote napkin notes for his daughter and tucked them lovingly into her lunchbox every day. When he was diagnosed with cancer and learned that he might not live much longer, he decided to write enough napkin notes for his daughter that she could continue to have a note in her lunch box each day until she graduated from high school.

I was so moved by this simple but remarkable gesture that I decided to use the idea to connect with several of my students over the holiday break. During the two-week holiday breaks in Virginia, students are away for over 400 hours, so writing short notes to my students during this time was a perfect way to bridge the gap between home and school and remind my students that I was thinking of them. I made a special trip to the post office and bought a variety of fun, kid-friendly stamps. For stationery, plain but brightly colored notecards and matching envelopes did the trick. The notes I wrote were not long, but they were thoughtful—I was careful to include personal details and to ask specific questions.

The notes were the first thing every student mentioned when they arrived back at school after the break. Some were laughing at my atrocious artwork that I'd included with some of my notes, some couldn't wait to answer the questions I'd asked. And every one of them came back to the classroom with a huge smile on their face. Holiday mission accomplished!

Chip and Jo

My wife loves our children, her family, our dog, the house, cooking, and watching Chip and Jo on *Fixer Upper*. I fall somewhere below "swiffering" and cleaning the fish tank, around 16th on the priority list. *Fixer Upper* is a fascinating show. It's fun to watch the process of remodeling a home and then decorating it, especially with a bunch of stuff we would love to have in our own home. But my favorite part of the show is seeing how much the renovations cost. To remodel two bathrooms, completely renovate a kitchen, add new windows throughout the house, and replace the roof somehow only costs $15,000 in Texas. How is that possible? I sometimes write down all the renovations and costs as seen on the show, and then call a business in Richmond to get a price quote on those exact renovations for our house. Once armed with an actual (and sobering) quote, I will send the realistic renovation cost to my wife to try and curb her enthusiasm for fixing different things in our house.

This might be one of the reasons why I'm 16th on the priority list.

But even if you're not Chip or Joanna Gaines, holiday breaks are still a perfect time to do a "Chip and Jo" renovation project at your school. I have been lucky enough to work with some amazing and thoughtful parents, and over one holiday break, a group of parents remodeled the faculty lounge and bathroom. They added a beautiful countertop and backsplash in our kitchen area, painted, hung up curtains, added a new couch cover, and decorated the walls with framed photos. Chip and Jo would have been proud.

Over one holiday break, I hired an artist to paint murals throughout the school in order to bring blank spaces in our building to life in vibrant and spectacular ways. It's also easy and inexpensive to host "painting parties" when students and parents join together to paint classrooms or staff bathrooms. Adhesive vinyl letters and designs are an easy and inexpensive way to add décor or an inspirational quote here and there as well.

I was able to get an Eagle Scout to build a wooden octagon-shaped pit for our students to play the fast-paced recess game called gaga. A Girl Scout troop designed and installed an outdoor learning classroom in order to receive their Silver Award recognition. A church volunteered to hang flags in our cafeteria of the colleges that our teachers attended. A local nonprofit organization painted motivational quotes in the student bathrooms.

There are plenty of powerful projects that can be completed over a holiday break, and if you need ideas, just turn on HGTV.

"Teamwork is the ability to work together toward a common vision, the ability to direct individual accomplishments toward organizational objectives. It is the fuel that allows common people to attain uncommon results."
—*Andrew Carnegie*

Holiday Tip-Off

If you had to estimate how many parents of your students were teachers, what would it be? Twenty-five percent? Ten percent? One percent? At our school, fewer than one percent of our students have a family member working as an educator, which typically means our parents need to work during our school holiday breaks. Daycare centers are currently making a killing during this time, which means it is costly for those families already struggling to make ends meet. My solution is this: run a holiday camp at half the cost of daycare. Parents would absolutely love the price and would practically break down the school doors to be a part of your camp. I know my wife would be one of the first in line.

If you ran just a four-day camp for $100 per child and got 100 kids to participate, you could put $10,000 towards new murals in the hallways, classroom enhancements, a research-based reading intervention program, or even a Kindle for each classroom. If you got 300 kids to participate, you could purchase larger items like playground equipment or solar panels to power your indoor garden or STEM lab. I know that if I increased our holiday camp attendance to 300, I would take my rising fifth-grade seniors on a weekend bonding trip to a destination outside of Virginia two weeks before school begins. I would use this "mission" trip to foster meaningful relationships among my students and, most importantly, to provide students with an experience that would enhance their leadership, communication, critical thinking, and problem-solving skills.

If you decide to run a holiday camp, I encourage you to reach out to local and nationwide businesses for financial donations. With a little extra money, you could order t-shirts and wristbands for your campers.

Students at our camps love when we bring in inflatables or a game truck that is loaded with video game systems. Over the past few years, I have found that the key to a successful camp is keeping your volunteer staff happy, which can be difficult during the holiday break! Therefore, bringing in food for your staff is essential. We've had Panera Bread, Starbucks, Dunkin' Donuts, and Krispy Kreme donate breakfast to feed our high school and college volunteers. Your PTA could even sell food during lunch to the campers as a PTA fundraiser. If you're looking for an incentive for your staff, offer scholarships for your teachers' children to participate as campers.

Holiday camps are an especially great opportunity to connect with your students who may have fewer opportunities for engagement. I can guarantee that any student would be ecstatic for the chance to be involved in sports, STEM activities, team-building games, arts and crafts, drumline lessons, etc. over the break. Each teacher can nominate a selected number of students for a camp scholarship, specifically those who would benefit from getting outside of the house. My hope is that our camps can one day bring in enough money to provide one or two college tuition scholarships that alumni from our elementary school would be able to apply for each year. As you can see, camps are a big win for all parties involved.

Be Upbeat

What do your students do during holiday breaks? Do they travel? Do they visit parents they don't normally live with? Do they receive any presents? Do they watch a ton of TV or play hours of video games? Are they left at home alone for most of the break because a family member has to work? Do they get three meals every day? Do they have to switch houses on Sundays? These are important questions to consider before posting on Facebook how excited you are to be away from school for two weeks. I can guarantee that all of your students are not going to have a "Disney" vacation during this time. This is why it's essential for educators to find a simple and upbeat way to connect with their students over the holiday break.

Over holiday breaks of the past, I have designed a set of postcards on Vistaprint.com for $12.99 and mailed one to each student's house. I have sent short and upbeat emails, but I think the students and parents appreciated my phone calls on the home line even more. I have scheduled an online chat and asked 10 trivia questions to keep my students sharp over the break. I even mailed a holiday card of our classroom family to each of my students' homes to remind them how much I love coming to school each day and seeing them there.

I have also made several home visits over the break. I always try to bring something with me, whether it's cookies or my wife's incredible wild berry homemade pie. Recently, our generous and energetic administrative team at Greenwood Elementary School delivered pizza to 10 randomly selected families on a snow day. Over spring break, we once stuffed 10 large Easter eggs filled with non-peanut treats and mailed them to families through UPS. The local middle school principal and

I even met at a park and took on some of our students in an intense basketball game.

Before one particular spring break, I hosted a leadership team meeting. I was in the March Madness mindset, so I gave each grade-level chairperson and administrative team member a blank 16-team bracket. I asked the leadership team to write down 16 people who worked within our school but were not on our leadership team. They could select teachers from any grade level, bus drivers, cafeteria workers, custodians, etc. I then told the team to look at their brackets and select the individuals that would be the best at building student relationships over spring break. Getting through the first round was tough, but once they got to the final four, powerful conversations were being held about why this person would be better than the other. By the end of the activity, we had a well-thought-out list of influential people in our building and an impactful list of ways to connect with students over the holiday break.

What if you created a scavenger hunt for your teachers on the last full day before a break? Cut out shapes of turkeys, snowmen, elves, Easter eggs, and bunnies. Ask your administrative team to write the name and phone number of a student who would benefit from a teacher connection over the holiday break on the back of one of these thematic cutouts. Then hide the cutouts throughout the building (alongside a Target or Starbucks gift card) and turn the teachers loose. When the teachers find the mystery item, not only would they receive a well-deserved treat, but they would also be responsible for making a connection with that student over the holiday break. How powerful would it be for a student to hear from a teacher they may or may not know? This is how you keep students (and teachers) upbeat and heighten a sense of community and connectedness.

I absolutely love the holidays because it's a wonderful time at home for my family and me, but I know that many of my students need to be uplifted during this time. By visiting the homes of such students in order to connect, catch up, or just play board games with them, you will create a memory that he or she will never forget. Even just getting something in the mail may provide a much-needed lift. Continue to be upbeat for your students, and let your light shine, so that it may serve as a beacon for them throughout the year.

"Imagine a world where people wake up every day with the knowledge that they matter."

—*Garth Callaghan*

Summer

Wayne

"Stop, look, and listen."

I am proud to be from the great Garden State of New Jersey. But when people hear me talk, they often think I'm from rural Alabama. Since I have been living in Virginia for the last 17 years, I have acquired some strange Southern twang mixed with my New Jersey accent that makes saying *water, coffee, dog,* and *drawer* almost unbearable. When I sing, I think I sound like a combination of Lisa Loeb and Robin Thicke but have been told it sounds more like a combination of Eeyore from *Winnie the Pooh* and Herbert from *Family Guy*. Needless to say, my dreams of picking up ladies on karaoke night have never came to fruition.

I am proud to have been raised in a beautiful town called Lawrenceville, also known as Exit 7. Lawrenceville is about 30 minutes from Philadelphia, 50 minutes from New York City, an hour from the shore, and an hour and a half from losing $500 on the blackjack table in Atlantic City. In Lawrenceville, we have the best bagel shops and pizzerias, but Starbucks cafés are scarce. We do not pump gas, and we drive maniacally through all of our roundabouts.

Growing up in Lawrenceville, I was blessed with an amazing family that I continue to look up to daily. Yes, my folks went through a very difficult divorce, but I imagine most divorces don't end in sunshine and rainbows. My parents' relationship struggles made me a better parent today. The one constant throughout the more tumultuous times was their love for my brother and me. My parents attended every sporting event and school conference. They scolded us when we made horrible choices, provided encouragement when needed, and taught us the importance of giving back to the community. Even now, my mom and dad continue to lead by example, and if I can be half the parent that each of them has been to me, I will call myself a successful father.

One of my mother's strongest attributes is her love of helping others. She worked and volunteered in the nonprofit world for over 20 years. My mom raised funds for the American Heart Association and the American Cancer Society through special events, grants, major and planned gifts, and individual gifts as well as corporate and community donations. She also cheerfully provided transportation, blankets, food, and, most importantly, tons of love for patients going through chemotherapy. My mom has always wanted to make a difference in the world, and whenever she is presented with the opportunity to make a positive impact in someone's life, she accepts it with open arms and an eager heart. It was because of my mother's unending compassion that when a student who had moved to our town from Atlantic City became homeless, we welcomed him into our home without hesitation.

His name was Wayne. I was a 6'1" gangly sophomore in high school, and Wayne was a 6'3", 185-pound, African-American junior. The way he walked and talked was smooth. Wayne took great pride in the way he dressed and would spend 20 minutes ironing his basketball uniform. A little much if you ask me, but the girls absolutely loved him. I was more like an awkward giraffe, who sometimes tried too hard by wearing hand jewelry and a leather jacket. But we both loved '90s R&B music and to work out every morning before school. And before long, we literally did everything together: basketball, movies, parties, studying, double dates … you name it, we were together. It felt like I had gained an older brother.

During the weeks I was away at my dad's house, Wayne stayed at my mom's and completed his chores or helped with dinner. He kept his room tidy and cut grass on the weekends to earn some shopping money. My mom met with Wayne's teachers and assisted him with his projects and homework. Wayne joined in several community service projects with my family. We participated in a race that supported the fight against breast cancer. We assisted with the set-up for a gala in Princeton. But what Wayne loved the most was giving food and clothing to the homeless in Trenton, New Jersey. And our family loved Wayne.

Toward the end of May, Wayne was notified that he would be living with his grandmother in Atlantic City for the summer, since she needed his help around the house. This news dramatically changed Wayne's demeanor. For the final few weeks of school, Wayne became quiet and reserved. He lost interest in participating in activities outside of school with my brother and me. He isolated himself in his room and our relationship deteriorated. Wayne shut down. School ended, and Wayne moved to his grandmother's house—but he never came back. I never heard from him or saw him again.

I think of Wayne often, and keep him in the forefront of my mind—particularly when the school year begins to wind down, and my staff and students are looking ahead to summer. What I learned through my experience with Wayne is that summertime can be difficult for many students. Wayne's engagement plummeted toward the end of the school year, just like I have seen in many children I have worked with since then. Many of them become preoccupied with worries about the inconsistencies and uncertainties that the summer will bring. In some cases, the structure and consistency that school provides are the very things that make the difference between a child being receptive to learning and personal growth, or just flat out giving up and shutting down. For some children, school is the only place they can count on to provide breakfast and lunch on a daily basis. For some children, having access to supportive adults like their teacher or school counselor is what gets them through the day. School staff and administration can also play a vital role in child and family advocacy or serve as mediators between non-communicative parents. School is often the place a child goes when parents work overtime and double shifts to make ends meet.

What happens to these kids during the freefall of summer? Are there ways we might step up to make things just a bit easier for these children? During the last week of school, I strongly encourage you to be hypervigilant while observing any shifts in your students' behaviors. Monitor students' emotions: are they exhibiting anger, fear, or sadness? Turn off the videos and continue to build authentic relationships with these children. Ask your students questions and pause as you genuinely listen to their answers. Try to avoid posting countdowns to summer break on your social media platforms—some children don't want to be constantly reminded that the action-packed school year is coming to an end. Every year at Greenwood, when that last bell rings and many children are happily rushing to the bus loop, there are always some children who cry and hold on tight to their teachers. In your understandable excitement for summer to begin, just remember to tread lightly with these little ones.

This chapter discusses some of the ways you can help make this time for your students memorable, happy, and even productive, as you edge closer to summer break. Stop, look, and listen, and I bet you will find one or two "Waynes" within your family of students.

Final Countdown

I f you had to use a word to describe the teacher morale and school climate the last week of school, what would it be? I'm guessing you would use words like *cheerful, radiant, carefree, energetic, joyful, ecstatic, upbeat, delighted,* or even *chirpy.* Over the past 14 years in the education field, I have come to recognize two distinct categories of teachers during the last week of school.

The first group I call the "pack and go" crew. The members of this group usually begin their countdown to summer on social media right after spring break, posting a constant thread of end-of-school-year memes. Admittedly, I've enjoyed my share of these, and humor is essential in this profession! However, these teachers typically use the last week of school to play movies for their classes, so they can focus on packing up their rooms and stuffing report card envelopes. On the last day of school, students enter a classroom with the walls completely covered up by bulletin board paper and the desks and chairs stacked neatly in the corner. Students sit on the floor and sign each other's yearbooks for three hours. As soon as the students are gone, so are the teachers.

The second group of teachers are the ones who continue to roll forward with creating a magical educational experience until the very last minute. They bring out their STEAM projects, solar cookers, and code robots to race through a maze. They harvest the outdoor garden and have a salad party. They make their students crack codes, discover clues, and solve puzzles in order to "escape the classroom." These teachers start hot topic debates that involve collaboration, communication, research, critical thinking, and problem solving. These teachers have their students perform a "reader theater" with parents invited into the classroom. These teachers have what I call the "It" factor, because they are searching for the Waynes of the classroom and squeezing the maximum potential out of every single minute during the final countdown.

As a classroom teacher, I took the final countdown very seriously. Each year I researched innovative projects to implement during the final week of school. I never wanted to rest or show a movie. I treated the last week as the last time I would ever have these children in my classroom. Therefore, whatever we did, it had to be something that would leave a positive imprint.

One of my favorite end-of-the-year activities was called "The 20th Reunion." My students had to write a three-minute speech as if they were 20 years older. Students shared the college they attended, the dream job they landed, and, in some cases, the family they had begun. In the speech, they had to share a few memories from our classroom "20 years ago" and thanked all the people who helped them achieve their dreams. These speeches were powerful and led to many tears for the students, parents, and especially me.

To make this event even more special, I asked all my students to dress in formal attire and invite their parents and grandparents to attend. I decorated the room with balloons and confetti. One year a parent went all-out and designed a beautiful cake for the event (which I had to sneak past the principal since food was not allowed into the school at the time). We sang a few songs, gave a ton of hugs, smiled, and laughed. I plan on sending them their speeches when they graduate from high school, to remind them of the goals they set in my classroom, eight years before.

The last couple weeks of school is also a stellar time to help children further develop "soft" skills. Soft skills are personal attributes that enable someone to interact effectively and harmoniously with other people. As educational systems rely more heavily on integrated technology and look to accommodate the burgeoning presence of online learning communities, the ability for students to know how to effectively communicate and collaborate with their peers and teachers is crucial. The possibilities are endless, limited only by our imaginations. One project in particular was a huge hit with my students: they were challenged with the task of writing and producing a rock album. All albums had 10 songs, each highlighting a special event from our year together. They had a blast designing their own album covers, writing lyrics, and performing their songs with their bands. There are a number of digital platforms around now that would lend themselves beautifully to this endeavor, like Flipgrid. The point is to help and encourage students to be excellent problem solvers and critical thinkers, which will make them adaptable learners who are ready for 21st-century classroom experiences—and beyond that, 21st-century careers.

As an administrator, I still try to make the final countdown a magical experience. We hold pep rallies, award ceremonies, and grade-level performances. We organize a Challenge Day where second graders take on the third grade, and the fourth graders compete against fifth graders in a series of field day games, to determine who is the top dog in the building. There are no ties. We have career day, Junior Achievement, a stock market tournament, and a Math 24 competition. We've organized a Moving Up Day, where students spend a few hours with the teachers from the next grade level to hear about their procedures, their expectations, and the thrilling projects they'll be completing over the following school year. But my favorite activity is the fashion show.

The fashion show is a great opportunity to highlight the talents of the more style-minded people in your building. This past school year, JCPenney invited 10 selected students to shop for four outfits each to model at school. A local church provided our teacher volunteers and students with transportation, and we shopped until we dropped! The students showcased their new outfits in front of the entire school on the morning announcements the following day.

This school year we are hoping to host a runway-style event where students and teachers model some of their favorite outfits after their visit to JCPenney. An emcee will provide commentary and play some music while strobe lights and a disco ball provide the lighting. We will even host a community bazaar where students and teachers can sell jewelry and clothing they have designed themselves.

The idea of hosting a yearly fashion show came from my experience in New York City as the winner of a teacher makeover from Jones of

New York. Five teachers were selected from across the United States as the top educators of 2012. A limo service provided transportation, I sat front row at the "Rock of Ages" show on Broadway, we ate at the best restaurants in the city, unlimited wine was provided by the hotel, and we each had a fashion consultant for our $3,500 shopping spree at Macy's. I can still remember the excitement of walking into Macy's, two hours before it opened to the public, with an entire film crew behind us. I felt like an absolute rock star. After hours of trying on clothes and getting all selected items altered right on the spot, we headed to the *Rachael Ray Show* to reveal our outfits, and then to a photo studio to take professional portraits.

What an unforgettable moment. This trip made such an impact on my life, which is why I will continue to host a fashion show at my school. I want the students to have the same feelings I had in New York and experience the sense of pride I feel every day that I wear those outfits. Hopefully, one day in the near future, I can fulfill my dream of loading the hardworking and underpaid teachers and all other staff from my school on a bus and taking them on a $1,000 shopping spree. Corporate America, can you please make this dream a reality?

Impact Club

One of my college basketball teammates, Ryan Sloper, began a nonprofit company called the Impact Club that has made a major impact in Northern Virginia in only one year. Its mission is to "be the strongest community in every community." He gets at least 100 community members to commit to attending four meetings per year and donating $100 per meeting. At these quarterly meetings, three local charities selected by Impact Club members make a three-minute presentation as to why the members should give their donations to that cause. After the presentations, all Impact Club members vote on the charity that they feel most deserves the prize, and winner takes all!

Since Ryan launched his chapter in Northern Virginia, he has launched 13 other chapters throughout the U.S. and New Zealand. In 2019, he plans to launch 30-plus more Impact Club chapters with a projected donation of $827,600. He is making a difference in the lives of so many people.

Now I assume your school has either a PTA, PTO, or some type of booster club that raises funds to support your school's vision. But what if you implemented the concept of the Impact Club at your school, and had the students compete? What if you had 100 community members and parents donate $100 to become a member of this program? $10,000 can be an incredible incentive to motivate your students to complete an essay contest the last two weeks of school. The students would be challenged to write how they would spend $10,000 to make an impact on the entire building. If a $100 donation seems too high for your community, make it $25! A total of $2,500 could still make a huge impact in your school.

An essay contest is also a great way to gauge your students' interests and wants. Maybe the students would want to purchase water fountains to fill their water bottles, or a shade structure to cool down the playground equipment. Maybe they would like more iPads or computers in your STEAM lab or makerspace, or a TV for your cafeteria. Maybe they want a drum set for your hallway, a sound system for the auditorium, or to replace the old desks in a classroom with standing tables. This feedback from your students is essential and should play a major part in guiding your decisions for school improvements.

Once you collect all of the essays, teachers can vote for the top five essays at your end-of-the-year faculty meeting. This would provide a positive morale boost and would get the staff excited to come back to school the next year with some new improvements in progress.

Over the course of the summer, the administrative team would notify the five selected students about their essay making it to the final round. These students then have the entire summer to prepare a three-minute project proposal and persuasive speech. Students can use any method they choose to sway the audience's decision. They can use PowerPoint, storyboards, song, dance, etc. The floor is theirs. The administrative team can announce the essay finalists to the entire school community and send out an open invitation to cheer on their fellow classmates before the final vote.

The evening of the presentations, all 100 donors should be invited to sit in the front rows of the auditorium in their Impact Club shirts. Each student gives his or her three-minute speech, and the Impact Club members conduct a live vote for the winner. Present the student winner with a large check on the spot and post pictures of the event on the school's social media platforms, to motivate other community members and parents to be a part of the Impact Club next year!

The following school day, the administration can begin to implement the winning student's plan immediately. The PTA, PTO, or booster club could also reevaluate the four essays that did not win to determine if they still want to support those projects. This would be a great way to give your annual fundraiser or direct donation program a focus for the year.

"Crush the Slide"

This is the phrase that can be posted everywhere throughout your building as the summer break approaches. "Crush the Slide!" t-shirts could be created by your SCA and sold by your PTA. "Crush the Slide!" is what your teachers will yell to their students as they pass out enthusiastic high fives in the hallways. "Crush the Slide!" is what the student news anchors on your morning announcements will shout after a hype video is shown of the teachers and administrators destroying a Fisher-Price plastic slide with a sledge hammer. "Crush the Slide!" is a great way to motivate students to defeat the "summer (back)slide" that normally happens when they spend an entire summer forgetting everything they learned over the schoolyear.

The Crush the Slide program was hands down one of the most powerful events of the schoolyear at Greenwood Elementary. The day started off with each teacher splitting their classroom into four groups. Each group rotated to three different 30-minute rotations throughout the building from eight o'clock to ten thirty.

The rotations included the following:

Public Library Guest Speaker and Book Fair Visit

Students went to the school library at Greenwood to listen to a librarian from the local public library talk about their summer reading incentive program. The librarian shared pictures of the library's different sections and discussed the process of acquiring a library card to check out books. She also shared two dates on which our school would partner with the library to provide free ice cream to the Greenwood students who visited the library that day. Once the public library presentation was finished, students went to visit our Scholastic Book Fair for five to 10 minutes. Profits from the book fair went toward purchasing enough lumber to build a few Little Free Libraries to place in different areas of our community.

Book Camp Out

When students arrived in the gym next, the lights were off, stars were projected on the walls, and tents were set up throughout the room. The sounds of a campfire hissed and popped through the sound system. Students used flashlights to select three summer reads from bins of books donated by Goodwill. The students took their summer reads into a camping tent and read quietly. Parent and high school volunteers passed out s'mores to the students and even wrote a message in each of their books to motivate them to continue reading over the summer. What an incredible book camping experience.

Student-led Conferences

Parents were invited to school to attend a 12-minute "conference" led by their child about "crushing the slide." If a parent could not attend the student-led conference, a teacher, parent, or administrator volunteered to sit in, so that every child could speak to an adult. During the conference, students presented their favorite book, author, series, and genre. They shared their reading data from the past year, site word recognition results, language arts grades, favorite piece of writing, and reading level according to Fountas and Pinnell. The students then defined a "summer slide" and showed a graph that predicted their progress over the summer according to the summer slide pattern. Then students shared the strategies they would use to beat it and "Crush the Slide." They shared information about our summer reading incentive program and made a plan to read 20 minutes each night. They shared how they could access free online reading programs throughout the summer. Finally, students shared how they would know if they beat the summer slide by taking the Fountas and Pinnell assessment during the first two weeks of the following school year. If the students beat the slide, they would get to go down a humongous inflatable slide at a pep rally in the beginning of the school year and receive a sticker that said, "Slide Crushed." If you are concerned about the students that did not reach their goal, you could order a moon bounce with the theme "Keep shooting for the moon!"

With a creative theme like Crush the Slide, I was able to stay connected with our students over the summer in creative, fun ways. Our admin team and teachers went into the neighborhoods within our school community to pass out books and built and maintained a Little Free Library stocked with books donated by Goodwill. Students and teachers met up at Barnes and Noble to talk about books and peruse the latest releases. Students and parents were invited into our school library every other week to check out books. Our incredible teachers initiated several days throughout the summer during which the music was cranked up, snacks and drinks were passed around, and books were given out to students from our donated stash of thousands.

It's also possible to stay connected right from your own office or home! I recorded myself reading books out loud and uploaded them to our school's Facebook page. I had a blast posting creative pictures online and sent postcards with my face photoshopped onto Dwayne Johnson's body breaking a slide. I recorded a creative summer sign-off with the hashtag "Crush the Slide" for the Sunday phone messages I continued to send out to the Greenwood community. One summer evening, we invited students and parents to our playground to meet with their friends and go down an inflatable slide and a giant slip-and-slide if they were completing their nightly reading log.

And since our school logged more hours of reading than any other school in the Richmond area throughout the summer, I shaved my hair into a mohawk at our open house ceremony in August.

Slide crushed.

The Future

As a basketball coach, the summer provided me with the opportunity to travel with my rising senior student athletes to visit colleges. I have been on more college tours than you can imagine. I have eaten in over 30 campus cafeterias (which is dangerous, as many of them include a dessert buffet). I have slept in dorms and spent hundreds of dollars on hotel rooms, all because I believe it is essential to provide hope and aspiration in our students' lives. How many of your high school students have ever been on a college campus? Even if college is not a consideration, I feel that as an educator, it is our duty to show them that something as simple as a visit could change their future.

When I coached the varsity basketball team at Benedictine High School, I had a player named Nat. He was a quiet kid who led a really difficult life before he transferred to the United States. As a result, Nat seemed to have a chip on his shoulder, on and off the court. Even though he was a solid student academically, Nat was still uncertain about attending college. He was skeptical that he'd find a good fit for himself and was reluctant to explore his options. During the summer before his senior year, I was able to convince Nat to at least look at what some schools had to offer, and we visited several small colleges in Virginia together. I will never forget what I saw in Nat's eyes as we pulled up to our first campus: hope.

When we returned to Richmond, it was evident that Nat was impacted by our visit. He didn't spend time worrying about partying with his friends, but instead put in extra time with his books and working on his jump shot. He was focused and hungry for success. Nat's extra effort led to an incredible senior year, and he was accepted into several esteemed four-year colleges. Recently, he graduated from college and landed a great job in Richmond, Virginia. Best of all, he's lost that chip on his shoulder, and he seems genuinely happy. After a really rough beginning in life, Nat was able to overcome his challenges and accomplish things that he (at one time) never dreamed he could. I'm incredibly proud of the man that Nat has become.

What if each teacher from your school took two or three hours out of their summer break to make a visit that could impact a student's future? If you work at an elementary school, could you take a rising "senior" to an International Baccalaureate middle school? If you work at a middle school, could you take a rising "senior" to a high school with a specialty academic center that piques their interest? Many of our students don't even know these specialized schools or programs even exist. Provide hope for your students. Give them aspirations and high goals, and I promise you they'll rise to the occasion. You may look back on all your accomplishments as an educator to find out that a two- or three-hour visit during the summer made the greatest impact in all your students' lives.

Be Hungry

Summer! It's true that nobody loves summer more than educators. Summer allows teachers the opportunity to perfect their craft, attend conferences, read *Lifeline 65*, and come up with new and innovative strategies for developing authentic relationships with their students. Summer is a time for educators to brainstorm with other teachers and administrators on what worked last year and what didn't. July through August is the time period I like to call the "Process."

As a teacher, I loved preparing for the next school year. Everywhere I went over the summer, I carried a notepad for ideas I would like to implement in my classroom or things I could add to lessons to make them more impactful. In the car, I listened to podcasts by motivational speakers and educators in order to bring something new to my students the following year. I kept a yellow notepad next to my bed because sometimes the crazy dreams I had revealed a new way to teach a math or science concept. My girlfriend then (now wife) would always chuckle during our vacations, because every other guy was either at the swim-up bar, throwing a football on the beach, or working on their tan, while I was under an umbrella reading a fourth-grade historical fiction book and writing down rigorous question stems. "What reading level are you reading today?" she joked each morning of our vacation, and almost 15 years down the road, nothing has changed. I still look forward to reading my second-through-sixth-grade-reading-level novels on our family trips. I absolutely love the Process.

As a principal, July and August are still my favorite months of the year, but not because I get to relax. I actually put in more hours of work during the summer than during the school year. In my county in Richmond, Virginia, our schools are open from seven o'clock in the morning to five-thirty in the evening Monday through Thursday in the summer. When I come into work on Friday and Saturday, I have to bring two additional outfits because the A/C is not turned on and, in Virginia, it gets hot! (If you're asking yourself why I don't just work from home … you must not live with small kids at your house.) I work all those extra hours because I'm hungry for a successful school year.

Whether as a teacher or principal, I love planning and preparing. I love creating a master calendar filled with new events each year. I get excited to talk on the phone and set up specialized field trips. Adrenalin surges through my veins when I apply for grants that could bring in much-needed funding, since our school's budget seems to decrease each year, as demands and expectations continue to increase. I fill my calendar with individual meetings with community partners, parents, teachers, and even students, in order to get feedback and input on my preparation for the new school year. I use the summer as an opportunity to visit other schools, attend conferences outside my district, and do anything I can to see how I can improve as an educator and leader. To be honest, I often enjoy the Process more than attending the actual events during the school year.

In my experience, I have found that educators who disconnect completely for two months struggle to find that "perfect" school year experience. July and August are needed to reboot, but also to plan a truly magical experience for students. The demands on teachers during the school year have skyrocketed, and that demand always spills over into summertime. Hopefully, one day soon, teacher contracts will include pay for all of their work, especially during August, when professional development sessions kick into high gear and attendance really isn't optional, classrooms are prepped, and lesson plans are written. Try to be mindful of how you spend your time so you can maintain a healthy balance for yourself, your coworkers, and your students. Be the best at getting better. This is something Coach Mike Rhoades taught me. He taught me never to be satisfied with being average or complacent, and he has shown this within his own professional trajectory. I am immeasurably grateful for the lifelines that he, Mr. Decrosta, and Ms.

Westhead threw my way. They would all tell you to stay hungry and remember what you love about being an educator. By investing your time wisely, you'll see a myriad of positive effects in your students.

"Motivation is what gets you started. Habit is what keeps you going."
—*Jim Ryun*

Back to School

Danté

"All the way up!"

Throughout my 14 years in the field of education, I have worked with so many amazing people. I am the person I am today because of those people who helped me along the way. Teachers, nurses, custodial and maintenance staff, cafeteria workers, and administrators have all played a major role in developing the passion I bring each and every day toward making a difference in the world. I am forever grateful.

I'll never forget my first teacher interview at Pole Green Elementary School in Hanover County, Virginia. I was 22 years old and eager to set the world of education on fire. I spent hours—as a matter of fact, days—preparing for what I hoped would be my first step into the field of education. When I arrived at the school, I was literally shaking with excitement, anticipating this potential opportunity. Pole Green's staff and students are known as the gators, and I was ready to order a gator tie, gator socks, even a green suit covered in gators. A few minutes after my arrival, the principal took me into an empty conference room with no interview panel. He proceeded to ask me only four simple questions, which took less than 10 minutes to answer. Then he stood up, shook my hand, and told me he would be in touch.

As I left, I was thinking to myself that this had to be the fastest interview possible. Heck, when I interviewed to be a lifeguard as a high school freshman in New Jersey, I went through a more in-depth interview process. Either he really liked me, or he really had to use the bathroom. About 25 minutes later, I got a call from the principal as I was at a Wendy's drive-thru to reward myself with a juicy chicken sandwich and a Diet Coke. In a soft voice, he kindly notified me that I did not get the job. When I asked what I could improve, he said, "I am concerned with your capability to build relationships with students."

I dropped my phone under the seat in my car. I paid for my food but drove off before I got the sandwich and drink. I was stunned. I thought building relationships would be one of my greatest attributes as an educator. This feedback hurt. Badly. But I used this failure to further fuel my passion and prepare for my future interviews.

My second interview was at Echo Lake Elementary School, the home of the dolphins. I was not as thrilled about the possibility of purchasing dolphin attire, but that did not deteriorate my enthusiasm for the interview. The minute I walked into that school, I felt something I hadn't felt at Pole Green: an immediate connection. Everyone was warm and welcoming, and seemed genuinely excited that I was there, from the office staff to the interview panel. Someone even slipped me a bottle of water as I was ushered into the conference room, where my future hung in the balance. The sense of connection I'd immediately sensed, along with the small kindnesses extended my way, seemed like signs portending a positive outcome, and my hope blossomed. Feeling strictly at ease and fully in my zone, the interview began.

I nailed it.

As I drove to my next interview, I received a call from Echo Lake Elementary, with a job offer and a request to not attend the next interview. I accepted the position and changed my driving route to Wendy's, which would soon prove to be two of the best decisions I have ever made.

Echo Lake Elementary School is a magical place, and an incredible community filled with passionate educators. My first few years of teaching, I was in "sponge mode" as I constantly observed my coworkers and the way they spoke with their students and parents. During my planning period, I frequently observed the best teachers' lessons in order to learn their classroom management strategies or how they differentiated instruction to meet the needs of all their students. In-depth conversations with my coworkers contributed to the culture, content, understanding, and skills necessary for the progression of 21st-century skills in my classroom. Every day was a learning experience, and I was learning from the absolute best.

I had the privilege of teaching at Echo Lake Elementary for five years, and then I decided to transfer to Pinchbeck Elementary School to gain a different teaching experience and continue to grow as an educator. I'll never forget how excited I was to meet the students, families, and teachers within this new community, but how nervous I was about making a great first impression. So I arrived extra early that summer to set up my fish tank, picture collages, stereo system, and classroom library. I was determined to have my classroom completely set up so I could walk around the school and meet all the teachers during our back-to-school teachers' work week.

On the Friday before all the teachers would arrive the following Monday, I wanted to put a few final touches on my classroom; however, that day I was also in charge of watching my girlfriend's (now wife's) dog, Jake. Jake was a 90-pound Saluki-Greyhound mix who was not very friendly. He was abused for three years before my girlfriend adopted him from a shelter and gave him all the love in the world. Even though Jake sometimes used the bathroom inside the house, barked at everyone walking past the door, cried during storms, and ripped up furniture on occasion, he was loved every minute of his life with us. He had his challenges, but I still thought it was a great idea to bring him with me to school, since nobody would be there until Monday.

When I got to my classroom, the room was extremely hot, but I was only planning on being there for about 30 minutes. As I placed all 24 back-to-school packets on each of my student's desk, Jake began barking uncontrollably. I looked around and didn't see anyone outside my window. I thought maybe a squirrel had snuck into my classroom since it was an outdoor campus, but I couldn't find one. I didn't know what to think.

Then suddenly, the floor below me jolted and the walls started to shake. It was an earthquake.

The shaking only lasted a few seconds, but it was a long few seconds. This was not a major earthquake, but since it was my first experience, a 2.5 magnitude shake felt like it must be a 10 on the Richter scale. As soon as the floors stopped moving, Jake and I got out of there and drove home. The rest of my classroom preparation could wait until Monday.

Throughout the weekend, the earthquake was the talk of the city. Everyone was wondering if school would be cancelled on Monday, and in some counties the damage was significant. But for Pinchbeck Elementary, school was still on.

On Monday morning, all of the teachers were on campus early setting up their classrooms. I parked my car and headed into my room. As I walked down the hallway and got closer to my room, I noticed several teachers waiting by my door to introduce themselves. This school was going to be my new home, and I was so happy to meet my new teacher family ... until I opened my classroom door. As I pushed open the heavy wooden door, a horrible smell poured outside. It was like something was dead in there. These teachers who had been welcoming me with a smile now looked at me in disgust. They rushed away and I turned to find out what happened. As I slowly walked to the corner of the classroom to turn on my lights and the A/C unit, I stepped in something squishy. That's when I realized what happened: Jake pooped in my classroom.

The chance for that great first impression I was hoping to make was long gone. My foot was covered in poop and my classroom plugins couldn't help the smell.

Even though this was not a dream start, it was a dream three years teaching at Pinchbeck Elementary School. It's tough to put into words how grateful and appreciative I have been for the opportunity to work side-by-side with some true miracle workers of education.

For my ninth year in education, I took a job as an instructional technology resource teacher and traveled across the county to all 44 elementary schools, to provide innovative digital learning lessons on computers and iPads to thousands of students and teachers. This position also provided me with the opportunity to work with many knowledgeable principals, which encouraged me to take a step into the dark side: administration.

Two years after serving as an assistant principal alongside a passionate principal and mentor who was herself a gifted educator, my dream came true: I landed a principal position at Greenwood Elementary School. And guess what? Greenwood is also the home of the gators! I was finally able to purchase those gator ties and socks (although I still haven't found the green gator suit). I was more determined than ever to make the best of this opportunity. I wanted to make a dramatic increase in test scores and reduction in discipline, but I knew it all started with building relationships, the lifeline for success. My first day in the office on July 5, 2016, I did nothing but plan events to connect with our community.

Out of all the events I organized throughout July and August, one of the most engaging events was our community bus tour. Greenwood staff, about 85 in all, piled into two extremely hot yellow school buses during their first week back at school. We ventured to six designated bus stops with an arrival time that was provided to our community weeks in advance and posted on social media platforms. The teachers and staff screamed and cheered while we drove through the community with the windows wide open. When we arrived at each bus stop, our school staff (teachers, librarians, nurses, custodians, and office workers included) rushed off the bus to high five all the students and parents who were waiting to meet us. We took group pictures, talked, and laughed.

The second year we took our community bus tour, we amped it up even more. We brought drumsticks and orange five-gallon buckets from Home Depot. Teachers brought snacks, ice pops, and school supplies. We borrowed "Big Blue," a bus from the department of family engagement, to follow us and pass out school supplies and back-to-school clothes. We even had two film crews follow us through the neighborhoods. They turned the footage into a hype video for the school year called "All the Way Up!" so our whole community could see the excitement we had to have our students back at school. The excitement and enthusiasm from the teachers on these few first days set the tone for the entire year.

As we pulled up to the school after our bus tour, I looked closely at our staff on the bus. They were sweaty, hot, sticky, exhausted, and probably completely stressed about setting their rooms up for our open house in only two days. But they were all smiling. There was a sense of pride and excitement for the lives they were about to impact. There was this positive glow gleaming from their faces as their heads nodded with approval and satisfaction. The reason why this was such a meaningful experience for everyone varies, but I can assume the joy they saw on their past and future students' faces had something to do with it. Maybe taking the first steps to developing authentic relationships with their new students and parents played a part. For one of my closest friends and a member of our administrative team, the community bus tour reunited her with a student who presented challenges for her in elementary school many years ago, but this student made a point to seek her out and say thank you for making a huge impact in his life. Many of these teachers were smiling because they saw their Rickie, María, Bryan, Holly, or Wayne. For me, the community bus tour was tremendously special because of a student named Danté.

Danté was a hardworking fifth grader with the best attitude. He opened car doors, rain or shine, giving out smiles and warm greetings each Friday morning with the Greenwood Gents. He used his basketball skills to pour in a few points against our teachers in the student versus staff basketball game. He assisted our garden club in taking care of our tower gardens and prepared school-grown salads for our students at lunch. He mentored kindergarten students as a member of our Buddies program, and since he had such a friendly personality, Danté was chosen as a member of our Friendly Helpers, who greeted school guests for career day, the Touch-a-Truck event, field day, and our end-of-the-year Moving Up ceremonies.

In the classroom, Danté was a passionate student who was eager to learn. He often asked his teacher questions in order to dig deeper into the content. He was selected by his teacher to receive a Character Trait of the Month award for displaying acts of kindness. His essay was selected and read at the fifth-grade graduation ceremony. Danté truly did it all.

Because of Danté's efforts toward making a positive impact in our school, he was one of the ten students selected for a JCPenney shopping spree during the final countdown to summer. When the students and teachers arrived at the department store, nine of the students headed in the direction of summer clothes. They wanted shorts, swimsuits, sandals, tank tops, or a LeBron James t-shirt. But not Danté. He headed straight to the suit department. He wanted to look his best when he read his essay aloud at his fifth-grade graduation ceremony. He selected an expensive all-white tailored suit that was *way* out of his shopping spree budget. But for Danté, the teachers and even some of the employees at JCPenney pooled their own money together to make it happen. That was a powerful moment.

Fast forward to a few months down the road. Our staff drove two school buses into the parking lot of Danté's apartment complex, banging on drums and shouting cheers out of the open windows. As I walked off the bus and was bombarded with student hugs and high fives, I noticed a young man standing on the curb wearing a white suit. It must have been 108 degrees outside with not one cloud in the sky to provide shade. Still, Danté had the biggest smile on his face. And when we made eye contact, he gave me a thumbs up and mouthed, "I'm ready for middle school."

My heart was full, and I couldn't wait to start the new school year.

Community Priority Workshop

Hosting a Community Priority Workshop is an absolute must. Whether you're a new principal, old principal, or a director at a daycare or church, a Community Priority Workshop is a great way to obtain feedback from your community in order to gauge what's working, what needs to be improved, and how to begin the process of developing strategies to get positive results. The Community Priority Workshop will serve to ignite the development of a collaborative and empowered school community. As a new principal, my Community Priority Workshop guided our school's focus and implementations for a successful school year.

The Before

Once you select a Community Priority Workshop date on a Tuesday, Wednesday, or Thursday evening during the summer, you will need to promote it. I recommend mailing newsletters to the entire community and posting your flyer on all available social media networks. Make personal phone calls to about 25 families and 10 teachers who are key players to your program's success. I would also follow up your phone calls by mailing a reminder flyer to secure their attendance (and don't forget to mail thank-you notes to those who show up).

Once you have completed the invite, you will need to identify two facilitators with whom your community members and current employees feel comfortable enough to be open and honest about the needs of your program. When I hosted my workshop at Greenwood Elementary School, I was lucky enough to have two principals from different schools lead my workshop, so I could stand in the back and just listen. By having non-biased facilitators, my workshop was very productive.

The last step of the "before" part of the process is ordering food and non-alcoholic drinks to keep everyone smiling! Put up some simple decorations and a few colored tablecloths by the food, and you are ready!

The During

On the night of the Community Priority Workshop, I welcomed all the parents in the largest space in our building, which was our gym. From the gym's center, I quickly stated that I was very excited to join the Greenwood community and was looking forward to hearing everyone's input. I introduced the facilitators for the evening, and then faded into the background to observe for the next hour and a half.

The facilitators reviewed the workshop purpose and procedures before splitting our large group into two smaller groups: parents stayed in the gym, and school employees went into the library.

Each group began the 30-minute session by highlighting the positives of our school for the first eight minutes. As parents called out an item, the facilitator wrote the ideas down on chart paper. When the timer went off, the facilitator reset it for 15 minutes. During this segment, parents stated all the things that needed to be improved within our school. (Make sure you have plenty of chart paper ready to go.) Once the 15-minute timer went off, each person in the room was given three dot stickers, which they then placed on the chart paper next to the items they thought were in most need of improvement. Each person could pick three different topics, or they could even put all three dots on one particular item. The timer for that phase of the evening was set for three minutes. Once both groups completed this process, parents and school employees met again in the gym. Each facilitator revealed their top three requested improvements.

The next step was for the facilitators to create two new groups by mixing up the parents and school employees. Once the groups were created, one group stayed in the gym, and the other went back to the library. A timer was set for another 15 minutes, and each group talked about the top six focus areas and why each one was important. After the timer went off, each person had another three minutes to choose their top three priorities. Once this process was completed, both groups came back to the gym to discuss the top areas of need.

To close the event, I thanked our facilitators for leading the workshop. I thanked the teachers and parents for guiding our focus for the school year and stated how I would follow up throughout the year to discuss what was to be implemented in order to solve our identified top three priorities.

The After

A clear and consistent follow-up is just as important as hosting an effective Community Priority Workshop. Therefore, I recommend sending a thank-you card, email, or phone call to all participants. Host a monthly Friday morning coffee chat to address your focus areas. At the end of each quarter, send a survey to all your stakeholders to gauge progress in tackling your focus areas and discuss your results with your leadership team. Additionally, in your monthly newsletter and social media posts, highlight the implementations that were put in place to turn your weaknesses into your greatest strengths.

Senior Camp

I t is true that when people feel appreciated, they will do more than expected. This goes for both teachers and students. Making others feel valuable is an essential and necessary component to achieving the highest level of excellence. This is why I firmly believe all schools should host a Senior Camp.

Senior Camp is a special opportunity for the oldest students in your building to come together the week before school begins. At my school, Senior Camp is for our rising fifth graders since our school hosts 700 students in preschool through fifth grade; however, a Senior Camp can and should be held for rising eighth graders (middle school) and 12th graders (high school). During this camp, our seniors complete a series of team-building activities, learn about our leadership clubs, and eat some great food donated by community partners. We have had motivational speakers and even the principals from local middle and high schools provide advice on "leaving your legacy" as a senior. Teachers and school counselors provide our fifth graders with mentor training as well as development on becoming the most effective campus leader. We have active breakout sessions where we compete in a variety of games including gaga ball, quidditch, team handball, and drumline practice. Finally, we complete our camp by hosting the same Community Priority Workshop with our students as we did with the adults, in order to see their goals and the areas within which our students want our school to improve.

My goal for our Senior Camp is to one day make it an overnight lock-in. With more time, our school would be able to split the boys and girls into separate groups and dive deeper into hot topics such as bullying, effective study habits, preparing for middle school, celebrating our diversity, social media expectations, and handling peer pressure. As a fifth-grade teacher, I participated in several overnight lock-ins with my students at the Science Museum of Virginia, and those classes were so close the entire year. As a basketball coach, I made sure my team participated in an overnight basketball tournament a few hours away every summer because I truly believed the time off campus would contribute towards building our family atmosphere.

Time with my students in the week before school started allowed me the opportunity to really get to know their interests, dislikes, past school experiences, and family background. All this information played a huge part in the way I taught my students and the incentives I provided. I firmly believe that our classroom produced high academic results because we had something many classrooms dream of having: we were connected. And when everyone is running on all the same cylinders, the sky's the limit.

Let It Glow

The last week of summer can be a powerful time to connect with your community. Instead of having the students return to school for the first time in three months just to pay fees, pick up textbooks, and drop off their $300 worth of school supplies to their new classrooms, what if you did something that truly got kids and their parents excited about heading back to school? What if you "let it glow" and hosted a Glowin' Moonlight Ride? Students, parents, teachers, and even community partners could meet at your school at eight in the evening with their bikes, and the school could provide glow sticks for everyone's spokes. Neon clothing, strobe lights, and portable speakers would be highly encouraged. Everyone would bike together through the community to let everyone know that your school is back in action.

If a bike ride wouldn't work in your community, could you host a Neon Fun Run? Participants could meet at your school as the sun is going down and run (or walk) a 5K around the track. You could give each participant a balloon with a glow stick inside to tie around their wrist, so they light up the entire track. The pep band from a nearby high school could play some jams while everyone runs around the track in their neon outfits. You could give out prizes to the most enthusiastic runners and a "no homework" pass for the entire school year to the student with the best glow outfit. That would create some serious excitement for the upcoming year!

Or how about a neon dodgeball tournament? Teams of eight could compete with neon balls in a gym full of black lights. Neon outfits would be a requirement. The winner of the tournament could receive a large glow-in-the-dark trophy and their name on a perpetual plaque in your Hollywood Hallways. A DJ could blast '80s music throughout the entire evening to really kick off the year in style.

If dodgeball is still not allowed in your school district, what if you hosted Glow Gladiators? Can you imagine how much fun your students would have competing against teachers and administrators in a series of physical challenges like in the popular '90s TV show—but with black lights? This event would sell out without question.

If no one in your community watched *American Gladiators* in the '90s, what if you hosted a Glow Dance Party? Music, some light snacks, glow-in-the-dark face paint, and zero slow songs are all you need to make this event a hit. If you want to go all out, you can add glow invitations, decorations, cups, glasses, ribbons, balloons, and even a chandelier made of glow sticks. If that's a no-go, your students could complete a Glow Escape Room, Glow Treasure Hunt, or even a Glow Obstacle Course. You could host Glow Bowling, Glow Mini Golf, or Glow Paint Night. You could even roll the dice and host a Glow Casino Night, Glow Mardi Gras, or play laser tag or paintball (just make sure you run these ideas through the proper channels, of course!). As you can see, there are many options to start the school year on a bright note. Let it glow!

Pops with the Principal

As a newly hired, first-year principal at Greenwood Elementary School, I was ecstatic to meet the students and parents of the community. I researched many different events that administrators across the country held during the summer to meet their community. I found a Principal Pool Party, but I didn't want to meet my community for the first time in a swimsuit. Poppin' Principal Party would have been fun, but I didn't want to expose my dance moves while making my first impression. I decided to go with a safer event called Pops with the Principal.

This event took place on the first Friday in August. I rented a Kona Ice shaved ice truck and anticipated purchasing about 100 servings. I hired a DJ to entertain the students with the "Cha Cha Slide" and "Cupid Shuffle." Students could play soccer with the new soccer goals I purchased over the summer, while I spoke with the families. I was prepared for everything except for one thing: the weather.

It was hot. And when I say hot, I mean a sweltering, humid, blistering, zero-shade, living-on-the-surface-of-the-sun kind of hot, and since this was the first time I was meeting the students and their families, I dressed in slacks and a long-sleeve shirt with a tie. I wanted to make a great first impression on my community; instead, I flat-out embarrassed myself.

The event started at six o'clock and there must have been a line of over 100 people already standing next to the Kona Ice truck. A huge crowd! I couldn't believe that many people wanted to meet me on a Friday night during the summer when it felt like it was 120 degrees outside. As I made my way to the front of the line, I felt sweat drip down my neck, face, back, legs, and arms. By the time I met the first four families, sweat was pouring from all areas of my body. I was sweating in areas I didn't even know could produce perspiration. My shirt and pants were completely drenched within 10 minutes, and worse yet, they had both become completely transparent. The striped print of my boxer briefs hovered just beneath the translucent film of my pants, leaving little to the imagination. In trying to stave off a full-blown panic attack, I attempted to breathe deeply, but ended up hyperventilating instead. I looked around to see about another hundred cars, filled with people anxious to meet their new school leader, pouring into the school parking lot. In that moment, I felt I had two options: run and hide in my office, door locked; or cancel the whole event and blame it on the dangerous heat index I'd heard about on the news.

Then a miracle appeared: my brother Matthew. He looked like a veritable mirage in the middle of my desert-hot soiree. Matthew had driven seven hours from New Jersey to support me for my first community event because he knew how excited I was. As soon as he arrived, Matthew rushed over to me and whispered in my ear, "Everyone can see your underpants." Under any other circumstances, I may have said something like, "No kidding, Matt." But I was in no position to be sarcastic when I realized that I was absolutely at his mercy to save me.

My brother and I hurried inside the school, and I told him that I didn't have any extra clothes. I was genuinely panicking. I didn't know what to do. Matthew looked over at me and said, "Take my clothes." Now, my brother is about five inches shorter than me, 60 pounds lighter, and loves to wear tight-fitting athletic clothing that highlights the fact that he runs marathons. Yes, Matthew got the better genes in the family. But there was no time to worry about all that. We traded clothes.

You might think that wearing an extremely tight t-shirt and tiny shorts would be the worst part of this outfit, but it was nowhere near as painful as trying to fit my size 12 feet into his size nine running shoes. I could barely walk. I could barely move my arms. I was miserable, but I had to get back outside to meet and greet my new community.

The second I went back outside, I got huge applause from the crowd. They didn't care what I had on. Right then and there at that moment, I fell in love with my community. I felt at home. I was officially a

Greenwood Gator! Despite the ill-fitting attire, I knew this new position would be a *perfect* fit.

As the event came to an end, I paid for over 600 cups of shaved ice and hopped into my car. When I was about to pull out of the parking lot, my brother's car pulled up next to mine. He was behind the steering wheel in our complete school mascot costume, Alex the Gator. Apparently he didn't want to wear my sweaty clothes home, and he borrowed the costume instead.

He rolled the window down and shouted, "Can't be shy on a Friday!"

Be Connected

As the summer dies down and a new school year springs to life, remember that trying just one new thing this year may be all it takes to find that pathway to authentic connection with your students. Just one moment of effort, one moment of humor, one moment of enthusiasm, can make the heartbeat of your school grow louder and stronger.

The beginning of the school year is an exciting time for many different reasons. Parents are ecstatic to get the kids out of the house. Teachers are anxious to see their class rosters. Bus drivers practice their route and anticipate the nervous looks on the kindergarten parents' faces on the first day of school. The cafeteria manager attempts a new recipe for spaghetti that the students will hopefully love. The custodial and maintenance team put their final touches on the building, and administrators typically run around the building like chickens with their heads cut off, making sure everything is perfect for the "grand opening." But not me. I grind all through July and August in order to sit back and relax on what we in Virginia call the open house. This is an opportunity for students to meet their new teacher and see the classroom before the first day of school. This is, without a doubt, my favorite day of the school year.

As a teacher, open house was the first time I had the chance to connect with my new students and their parents. This was the beginning of a new opportunity to be like Mr. Decrosta and change the course of someone's life. This was my first opportunity to be real and bold. This was the time for me to find my new Rickie, María, Bryan, Holly, Wayne, or Danté. This was the time for me to start my new classroom family.

As my new students piled into the classroom, I'd have a line of alumni waiting at the door. I smiled from ear to ear with pride when past students paid me a visit on this day. I loved hearing about middle school, high school, college, and their experience in the workforce. Former students sometimes brought in pictures of their dogs or girlfriends or boyfriends. Some students even had pictures from back in the day, when they were in my classroom. There were always hugs, high fives, and, in some cases, happy tears, because even after these students graduated from my class, we had remained connected.

Now as a principal at Greenwood Elementary School, open house still holds a very special place in my heart. I miss not having my own classroom family of 28 students, but now I have a school family of 700 students and about 100 educators, which is an amazing feeling—a multitude of students means a multitude of potential connections. Greenwood graduates come back and visit our teachers and administrators, and we all get emotional. Instead of standing by my classroom door, I now stand by the main entrance and welcome all of our new and returning families with the same energy and enthusiasm. I shake hands, high five, fist bump, and smile. I do it because I want to connect, and because I truly love working with these children. This year our open house took on a new dimension, and we added a dance party in the gym. After students met their teachers, they were invited to jam alongside a Bruno Mars and Motown cover band, while food trucks served up dinner in the parking lot. It was the best possible way to get our school year rolling.

But as the open house comes to an end each year, I have mixed emotions. I sit quietly in my office or classroom and take several deep breaths. The 65-hour countdown has now begun for another year. I can hear the clock ticking in my head and my heart begins to pound. My hands sweat and my legs bounce uncontrollably. My mind races, and I envision the year ahead of me and my school family. I can't help but feel overwhelmed at the weight of the responsibility. How will I connect this year? I try to settle down and block the noise, and my head fills instead with the clear dings of my wife's phone. I'm reminded that the true heartbeat of our school lies in building authentic relationships with our students, each and every day. The Lifeline 65 philosophy brings the focus of education back to where it should be, within the hearts of students. When educators work to build authentic relationships with their students and their families, the educational experience is transformed, and reaches far beyond test scores. Authentic connection can be a lifeline. It can save someone's life. It most definitely changed the course of mine.

Time moves too fast to wait. Jump in. *Ding.*

Connect with Me

Who has been *your* lifeline? Write their names in the 65, snap a picture and tag #Lifeline65 and @ryantstein on your social media platforms. I would love to get connected with my readers and see who has influenced your life.

Acknowledgements

I strongly believe that when you surround yourself with incredible people, you can accomplish the unthinkable. Over the past 14 years in education, I have been fortunate to have worked alongside so many incredible educators, and I am forever grateful for their support and inspiration. To my Greenwood family: thank you for being the life-line to so many of our "gators." You continue to impact my life more than you know. To my mom: thank you for showing me how to care for others. To my dad: thank you for showing me what it means to be a great father. To my brother and closest friend, Matthew: thank you for being one of the best people on this planet. To my stepmom, sister, grandparents, and in-laws: I love you with all my heart. To my wife, Kimberly: thank you for pushing me to tell my story and continuing to be the backbone of our entire family. To my children, Bryce and Bexley: I hope you get the opportunity to find a passion that brings you as such much joy as teaching and coaching has brought into my life. Your smiles and endless energy motivate me each day to get up early and be the best person I can be. To Jen Berdux: working on this project together has been a dream come true. I can't thank you enough for taking this risk with me as we work to expand classroom walls and impact more students.

—Ryan

In gratitude to Ryan Stein, who trusted me with his stories and gave me the opportunity and the privilege to help him tell them. Cheers, my friend. To my own personal lifeline, Virginia "Mumsie" Grohl, my tenth-grade English teacher and cherished friend: thank you for showing up at my gymnastics meets, inviting me to dinner, and taking the time to listen to what 15-year-old me had to say. You were demonstrating the Lifeline 65 philosophy way back when. To Cindy Patterson, my principal, prayer warrior, and friend: thank you for hiring me when I was called back to the classroom, and for giving me the chance to get back to my life's work with our KES Coyotes. Your words of wisdom, prayers, hugs, and constant support personally and professionally mean more to me than you know. To my parents, Dave and Melissa Costa, who have been my biggest fans since day one, and who have always encouraged me to write: thanks for everything. To my husband, my rock, Chris Berdux: thank you for your undying love and for your patience as I spent "just one more hour" in front of the computer. You are home to me. Finally, to my sons Nick and John Berdux: you will forever be my pride and joy. You have taught me so much about believing in myself. Thank you. I love you all.

—*Jen*

About the Authors

Ryan T. Stein has been recognized on a national scale as an Elite Educator and as a pioneer for student engagement, innovation, and achievement. As an educational songwriter and forward thinker, he sees no barriers. His high energy and contagious enthusiasm for building intentional and authentic relationships has created lifelines for school communities throughout Virginia. A devoted husband and father, Ryan likes to spend his personal time laughing alongside his wife, Kimberly, as they wade their way through the often-hilarious adventures of parenting their young son and daughter, Bryce and Bexley.

Educator, life-long learner, and dreamer *Jen Berdux* loves her work as a teacher at Kaechele Elementary School in Henrico County, Virginia. She lives in Richmond with her husband Chris, and is the proud mom of two adult sons, Nick and John Berdux.